Rooted In Grace
~ Medicine of Word ~

Poetry

Perry Annan Rose

Art

Amanda Burkman

In the writing

came the medicine,

in the reading

may there be yet more.

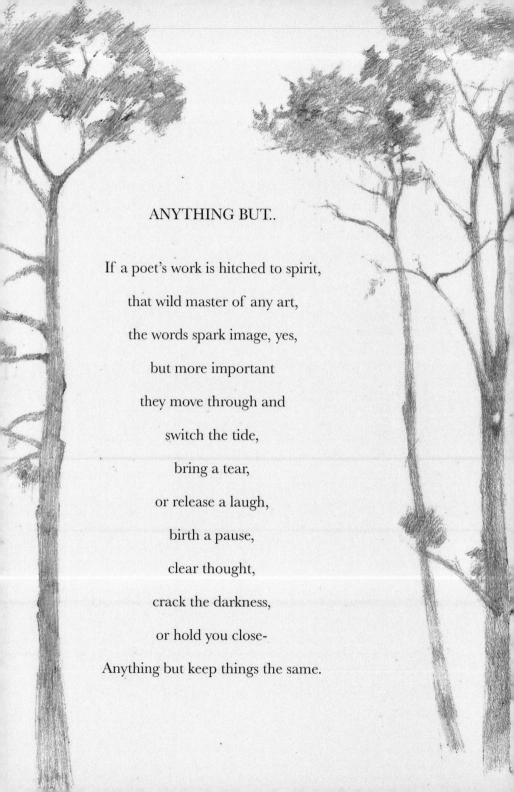

ANYTHING BUT..

If a poet's work is hitched to spirit,

that wild master of any art,

the words spark image, yes,

but more important

they move through and

switch the tide,

bring a tear,

or release a laugh,

birth a pause,

clear thought,

crack the darkness,

or hold you close-

Anything but keep things the same.

I COME BEFORE YOU

I come before you

Naked

caring not what you think,

whether my frown displeases you,

my tears scare you,

my laughter delights you,

my ecstasy draws you,

or that the tenderness of my heart

is familiar as the surface of the moon,

for we will all be dust in the end,

hopefully becoming,

long before that day,

not just fully alive but

luminous.

SENTINELS

up from the wet ground

atop the twisted arms of cypress,

two crows

sway

on needled fingers

brushing the sunrise..

with their black cutouts of sky

they look my way,

not bookends

but sentinels,

my return greeting

a blush of recognition

3 POEM DAY

at dawn,
hummingbird
atop the tree beside me,
singing singing..
enjoying her, i stand high in the pine
watching waves
pile
against rock.
chubby swell, at last-
what a winterless winter.

in rounded day,
crows feast,
the pasture their table.
waddling, hopping the lumps,
straddling gopher piles,
gaming each other
with territorial beak-nips of air.

following the disappearance of sun,
in the firesong above,
comes thousands of crows
-the local posse-
comical and loud,
holding their evening ritual,
flying southeast
to greet night.

a 3 poem day,
closing with red wine,
sewing together
the passing of light from yesterday
to today
into tomorrow

WORDS UNKNOWN

I hear the song you sing

even with words unknown~

In the tilt of your mouth,

the lift of your head,

the gentling of your eyes,

the blood warmth of your distant palms,

fingers circling in soundless emphasis.

I am One.

We are two.

Pulled together and moved apart,

like bees

loving the same flower.

Fragrance and color,

instinct and vision,

draw us to the ultimate..

In knowing nothing

we may experience All.

LET IT BURN

As feared,

the horse bolts the stable

while the house,

with towering eucalyptus growing in dry yard,

burns.

That horse- wild, ornery,

spirited and dismissive

of imposed boundaries-

his muscles work without strain,

his mind grasps

limitlessness.

Let the structure burn.

And jump

on the horse

who pauses only long enough

for you to turn as he passes and vault

onto his bare back,

feeling warm, sweated fur against naked limbs,,

Take hold,

weave fingers in knotted mane,

his tail twitches with fever to run.

Only one ride-

take it as far as it goes.

THUNDER AND VANILLA

I wept into that creek,

threw my voice into the forest.

Held by rocks, shoeless,

a mothering container of mountain

offered cracks of thunder,

and vanilla of dry ponderosa.

Here, by coyote's invitation,

song and word arose.

Safe to be cracked open,

the stars redefined boundaries,

bringing unguessable exploration

on two feet.

FROM THOUSANDS OF MILES

From thousands of miles

your kisses land

on my exposed skin;

butterflies, in their freedom,

multiply.

Three in the morning, lightning

thundered along the coastline.

And now, with bright sky,

rain falling in a wall

feet from none at all,

a rainbow.

Birds speak most in spring,

and the dreams, they gallop inward.

I bow to thee-

the jagged places only more to learn-

to soften, release, strengthen and trust…

It is your path I walk,

in you I am.

UNKNOWN FRIENDS

the flatbed tow truck

flies by on wet curving valley road,

my smile broad,

watching him go.

he has this highway memorized

just as i do

and the intensity of his focus

my match..

it's good knowing where we're going,

how to get there,

and having unknown friends along the way

STAY CLOSE

Cigarette smoke and cleaning chemicals
perfume the stairwell.
Head down,,
down down the black ledges to open pavement,
where bites
blue desert air.
Descending Bariloche's version of Lombard Street,
and entering the café,
a wood table for two seats one.
Segafredo Zanetti, and
leather placemat stitched in white
frame paper notebook.
Beyond the glass,
a couple
exchanges insatiable kisses
beneath red and blue road signs,
rubberbanding back to each other
following a single step of separation.
Hunger to touch,
to reestablish presence in form,
the gift of grounding through
skin meeting skin~
Delicious reminder we inhabit bodies,
Here,
in this moment,
in this place.
The rest, forgotten, a dropped definition.
Searching, grasping, holding,
it's dirt in wind,
diesel, hips on the rose,
and holes in which we stumble,
Celebration in a glance~
Stay close, there is more…

TOO

vinegary wine,

raunchy restaurant kitchen,

gum on sidewalk,

sand between teeth,

cracked mirror,

the last page, missing,

uneven stairs,

bitten nails,

oil-stained cloth,

thin walls,

mascara-lumped eyelashes,

static in the line,

half-inflated tire,

taxes,

and best bakery, closed;

it's all this too.

IN THE ILLUMINATION

In the Illumination
you will wriggle, tug, push free the skin-
your skin-
as, equally, it will be wrest from you.
In the remaking, upon looking down,
nothing remains.
And nothing is everything,,
What you thought was you,
as forgettable as spent tea-
grateful for the drink it provided, but done
so done.
With the infant sight
comes rearrangement
of place, purpose, person,
even in stillness.
Particularly.
While words fall short-
stones thrown across a chasm,
skittering the scree edge
and dropping-
Wait, just wait,
we'll join
where words are as unnecessary
as stopping the rain.

AND ANSWERS STILL

Beyond the most cherished,

what remains?

A fingertip pushes aside strands of hair,

Hummingbird comes to sit a breath away,

Two slow-dance, hidden among shelves of books for sale,

Blood moon, behind fog, suspends its wakeful,

And answers still;

The sweep of silence

grips,

unforgettable and impermanent.

Where can the spoken be formless

yet present?

Yesterday and tomorrow- never mind.

On the head of the pin,

alight,

an entire world widens before you.

THERE'S NO TELLING

travelers need not search for one another,

the finding is effortless.

as dust gathers on shoe laces

and tread wears to nothing,

we walk the same roads, admiring

the same blue.

i look, you see, earth rolls

through invented time and the incredible mastery

of chaos.

come to me. we are but flecks,

motes in sunlight, fragile

and measureless.

if my step and yours

coincide,

there's no telling

what we might become

AN ANCIENT IMAGINED SORROW

The loosening grip of an ancient imagined sorrow

frees up

the rolling giggles of a belly forgetting to stand sentry

against a world prepared to rip everything apart.

Annihilation lays waste to whatever weakens,

and the rebuild,

oh the rebuild,

brings unshakable footings,

windows welcoming sky

of blue and star and cloud,

and stained glass casting colored light in beams

where acoustics music cries to court

carry every soulful voice

to heavens protective

of all that's sacred and immortal.

WHERE NO THING MATTERS

Who ever taught you

your life is worth so little?

Not meaning your stuff,

your interests, your thoughts-

those are unimportant-

but You.

Life creates nothing less than Itself.

You shine

from your eyes, your smile,

each inspiration.

Where no thing matters,

we all meet here,

and the step of your bare foot,

the mark of your passing,

carries bliss forward.

Funny to question significance

of the rising sun.

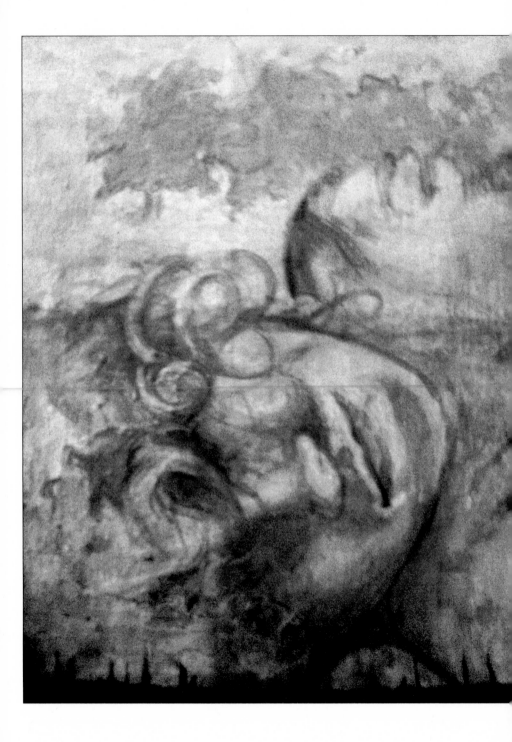

COME CLOSER

For every rejection

every refusal,

Say,

Come closer.

For every tear

and blemish

and tremble,

Say,

Come closer.

In jagged light when

all the the angles are wrong

and disheartening,

fall

in Love.

Be the tender one,

the present and caring one,

alone with yourself.

In that freedom

none can knock you from place,

your sway becomes a spin

becomes a leap

becomes a Song

to which others find

their own dance.

FALLIBILITY

As we watch

the magician's sleight of hand,

awaiting error

to show us his ways and fallibility,

the real show goes on.

Slow, slow,

sit and look from where the Paeonia scent

lifts out of sleep..

the ants gathering in the folds of petals

tremble in her grace,

walking their tiny regimented paths.

The swoop of sky above holds its breath,

wondering if today

the full bud will open.

SEA AND SKY

sea and sky hold to nothing

across and within them

Majesty has her way,,

the dashing and clashing

fold into rising color and lapping blue...

if water or ether

knew fear,

grasping would begin.

and no state of storm or still

could again be as free

as the liberated elements

giving endlessly

to all

who wish

to know beauty.

WATERS

We try

pushing away the waters.

Yet, there's no stoppable tide,

short of pulling the moon from the sky.

If birth,

then death.

When drawing this in

-with breath-

We are free,

-with exhale-

To take life's tender hand.

Precious day,

night's eggshell,

offers light exactly as long

as intended.

DIG IN

There is a dance

Between getting what we want

And not.

Often, not serves up the wonder-

What's a life that goes to plan?

Uncreative, controlled, missing the unexplained sparks,

a parched abiding, inviting scant vision, inside an airless cave.

Blasting past the walls

Free falling-

Rather to have an unexpected journey than the tourist package-

Come

Dig in

We'll get messy together.

SMOKE THICKENS

Smoke thickens-
the matter of lives, burnt.
Sky can't prepare for the soot
of curtain, letter, painting, bed pillow, tea pot, photograph,
weighting its blue.
Telling a friend his home is gone, eaten
by flames,
another unexpected duty.
Yet, mercifully, living words can be delivered
instead of the shock
of a middle of the night escape.
Drought.
Tinder.
Negligence.
Nature's force, fueled.
Green becomes black.
The redefinition of essential.
Memory reduces to what a mind can retain.
Celebrating moments,
understanding the past transforms,
in time,
like wood and metal consumed
by extreme and uninvited heat.
Humans skirt the fire,
narrowly-
for this, surging gratitude.
From the ashes,
magnificence does find grit.

"The Day Before the Lightning Struck"

June 2008
After the lightning struck, the Basin Complex Fire started.

UNTETHERED

there are times we must sit with all we'd rather run from.

taproot strength follows devotion to becoming

our honest, vibrant, untethered selves,

the ones clear as glacial streams, the true-hearted lovers of life.

few may understand us, making space for those who do.

joining our kindred brings brighter light to a world in utter need.

keep breathing,

this night will be day again soon and

much will be gained.

we are not alone..

TAKE THE HAND OFFERED

Imagining ourselves to be unlovable,
Knowing not our own expansive brilliance,
We swallow our own light
and hide in shadows of our own making.
Like a foot longing to be a fingertip,
loss.
And, at what cost? As we tumble up the first stair to the coffee joint..
How could the nose yearn
for the gifts of the ear
when perfumed steam from a cup of espresso visits
on its way to meet ether,
or when resting on the hair at the temple of our lover,
or sitting with a new book, cracking it to page one?
Had coyote visited but once before sunrise,
the turning of its rounded, black-tipped furry tail
would not have been paired
with a seated yawn-
a send-off into the riches of day.
Sometimes we like blindness
for its familiarity, yet
settling for impersonations of ourselves
robs this life of the jewel we each are birthed to be.
Let us take the hand offered,
enjoy coyote's satisfied yawn, and
erupt with a giggle at each reminder to stretch
into the Sequoian grandeur
of simply being.

PRAYER & LAUGHTER

Pine

Fog

Mournful owls~

Calling into darkness

none but echoes return.

The formlessness

of prayer and laughter,

what these hands care to hold.

Be still, medicine approaches,

no need to know how or when.

Listen,

the summoning~

UPWARD

Upward,
dry currents lift.
Time again for monarchs' return.
Riding autumnal air, they flirt
between grass heads and needle tips.

Seeking quiet,
I look for you---

In silenced effort,
you show your face-
everywhere.

Exhales weave, mine with yours,
warm braided through cool..
eyes closed,
skin registering breath of wind.

By abandoning the search,
I found you.
Life strips the longing,
beats out illusion's ache-
wool kilim struck until the dust stops rising,
clean,
lightened of the burden that never belonged.
Close to mind,
an ongoing remembering,
the weightless flight of butterflies
reclaims.
Orange and black paper wings.
Buoyant bodies feeding on flowers.
May we all be so lucky.
And,
in truth, We are.

BEAUTY WANDERS

Neither glabrous nor symmetrical,

lasting Beauty wanders

away from prescribed uniformity

and the wasted effort of rebellion.

In her,

the dynamism of bliss.

Fires consume obstacles, illusions

becoming the skeletons

of lace wings

honored in their sculptural ephemera;

in the end, they flutter,

blown free by breath

through gently pressed lips.

Light stretches into full expression,

at ease,

with plenty of room

to move.

FED BY SKY

Dismantling a life.

Kicking off old shoes,

the ones given-

once useful,

always ill-fitting,

finally worn through.

Taking bare to the contours,

sole to soul,

every granite nib and dusty stretch

fed by sky

and the penetrating scratch

of salt air.

Reaching beyond you,

I carry the minimum.

My skin soaks in what surrounds,

untouched by

what has passed or yet to be found.

I've wasted myself on an appealing lie.

These bright eyes aren't for any other

than this splash of sunshine

and that long drink of water.

Sand, trail, roadside-

Terrain changes

in winding tales.

Think I'll keep walking…

DAY DRESSES

Flying into morning,

garnet light

catches pine's reaching fingers,

Owl song becomes hawk cry,

Pale oat hears wind

and offers a sigh in return,

Drifting dream avoids the net..

Day dresses

and none shy away.

I HOLD THE FIRE

With your hand

touching my skin,

I see-

I hold the fire.

Through dulled eyes of regret,

my passion seems especially alluring.

But the spark you seek

another can not give you,

and mine's neither for sale,

nor being offered.

Your flame, faltering with pain,

requires tender attention

to feed it

with the missing joy you look outward to find.

Tend your own fire,

no one else can.

WITHIN REACH

Lift your palm,

kiss the center,

She waits there to kiss you back.

In your heart, She drums-

your pulse, Her rhythm.

The vision through your blinking eyes

of widest sky and massive cloud play,

that is She

gazing upon Herself.

Originating in you, or from the heavens- which?

Remember, One can not be outside itself.

She sustains, effortlessly

within reach-

You awaken

and Her breath is yours.

RAVISHING JOURNEY

In the moment you stopped

and saw me,

I knew Spirit was there

galloping between awakened hearts and keen eyes.

Explanations, unnecessary,

the impact of presence and recognition

loud.

We've both learned to ride

the untameable mustang-

no cloth. no leather. no fear. between.

With fur and flesh and speed and wind,

muscle gripping muscle, fingers laced in mane,

bodies leaping,

the greatest lone expanse breaks open,

a beauty possessing and unfolding into One...

Few comprehend where we have been.

In honor of sharing this ravishing journey,

thank you.

COHERENCE

Bleary-eyed.

Waves continue approaching shore-

Fuzz-brained.

Water breaks, endlessly, on stone-

Anxious-bellied.

Wind gathers east to west-

Rough-skinned.

Orchestra of silence in form

giving perfect coherence

to overcome

the small, blinding, and finite

with the unspeakably grand-

WITHOUT YOUR HAND.

How many pluck the thorn without the rose?

Dancers with hearts unmoved,

Climbers without grasp of height's uplift,

Farmers unpossessed by soil-

where are You?

Mystery awakens at the end of dream~

that sorrow and clamor you know

are not

the real movement.

The orchestra of a day,

rising sun, opening flower, resting dog,

starlight-

This play of life delighting any who see

goes on without your hand, or asking,

and isn't it miraculously so..

For any who stop and breathe and look

will find all the riches

are not only within,

but free.

BY FIRELIGHT

By firelight

the evening passes,

thoughts tumbling.

You come to mind,

wonder and smoke ascend.

Recalling the scent of you,

your curls between my fingers,

and the bright river we both ride…

Flame turns cypress to ash-

from beauty to beauty,

all things change.

IN THIS PLACE

Jump off the merry-go-round.

That common ride dulls the senses,

weakens the heart.

There's endless beauty

in walking the path with Beloved,

every step

discovery.

Depart from good and bad

wrong and right

righteous and evil,,

Find Love

in dawn's greeting,

the wind-sway of redwood,

breaking waves rolling white..

Beyond the two-sided trap,

One.

Here, resonant laughter visits often,

touch lingers into the unconscious,

and limits, like toppling dominoes,

care not for your fears—

In this place,

there are none.

BACK INTO THE WILD

I am the horse

being broken

back into the wild.

Forced bit

drops wet from mouth,

metal clanking,

rolling in dirt,

Reins under hoof,

Saddle scraped off

at the last tree..

Picking up

speed and spirit,

mane flying with wind and sky-

No destination

Clear vision

Feral reclamation.

IF THE TWITCH

If the twitch of a whisker

isn't enough,

Or leaping legs from one puddle

to another,

Or a droplet sliding down glass,

An exhale overheard from the next room,

A patch of sun on tile,

Late afternoon scent of wooden house,

Chocolate perfume from an unopened package,

First toe breaking hot bathwater,

Or fog rising, within grab, up the ravine,

Then what is?

Why the hesitation?

All lays before you

in the sublime light, and

quiet dark,

where even moon looks after you

while exploring the Unseen.

WHEN THE SHOW ENDS

I try to read

but fingers of morning light on the pines stop me.

And the clouds with holes

drifting eastward.

I'd take a call

but the juncos are talking

and hummingbird's sipping from purple flower head.

Try me later,

maybe when the show ends.

CENTER OF STORM WIND

Stand at the center of storm wind

bending blasting spinning...

Hair blows sideways with treetops and grass,

limbs clack over head, needles fly,

birds navigate through added force and necessity

Take off shoes, and penetrate that place

with your whole being-

offer dynamic quietude while the stir

carries everything away.

Let it move through you, alone.

THAT MOON

What's alone?

More than just you sits there

with no other humans in sight.

Life pervades.

Like now..

Fire, tea, words, the spiders in corners..

Flame talks with wood,

the heat of water and spice whisper to belly,

lamp light leans on white wall,

wool rug spreads reds and rose across the floor.

How could alone ever be?

Crickets surround both day and night,

and that moon

sure does get around.

UNION COMES ALONE

With fluid reach

cypress hold both the sun

and gathering birds giving audience

to dawn.

Union comes alone

not in the company of thought,

thought anchored by convenience-

convenient right and wrong, reliable should and shouldn't..

No and Union hear infinitely different music.

Moving to what the oak and crow listen to,

freedom arrives,

the controls of ethics not limiting the ability

to discern the sound of light and

feel the texture of color

painting the day.

RAPTOR

Laying this body down-
slumber denied, dream delayed-
she comes over me.

And I grow feathers.

From crown,
quills push through skin and
rush earthward..
flaring, fingering,
as ice crystals might broaden or scales overlap,
not resting upon but merging, rooting..
overcoming brow, eyelids now avian.
Beak descends, replacing nose.
Spreading downward,
feathering across shoulder
and ridge of limbs-
strong arm becomes stronger, lighter pinion.

Her penetrating vision. Her powered flight.
Protector and guide,
humility and respect give rise
to these wings.

REVERENCE SLEEPS

Past the noise,

reverence sleeps.

Stepping into silence,

we may rest with her

and the broken parts of us,

their voices will calm,

while divine nourishment

repairs us,

replacing tumult with Song.

YELLOWS BROWNS AND GREEN

Tall lush rounds wave-

no sound.

The lotus pond rests full with leaf and pod.

Frogs leap.

Up the hill,

dry corn and poplar

clap their yellows and browns.

Shooshing oak,

decisive beyond silence, still

holds to its green.

Owl and hawk

alternate the night with day,

same as home.

UTTER FEARLESSNESS

i stare at death directly

no barriers between us

blond predator eyes staring,

mine equally fiery, flashing

total dissolution

when and where we merge

i don't care

every day is life or death

the strangely ignored baseline

i'm stripped to bone

and nothing

except breath

separates us,,

in this death i now face

beyond it i see

utter fearlessness

SUMMONS

Walk into the fire.

Be purified.

Become water~

Wave through endless ocean.

Root in earth.

Mineral darkness feeds and holds you.

Breathe sky..

Fuel your own laughter and music.

Embodiment calls-

Burn brightly.

Now is your chance

to spend a lifetime

Rejoicing.

IN CROSSING PATHS OF CLOUDS

What the sheep dreams,

I do not know,

but the mirror of a day jumbles

and obscures

redefines and enhances,

so perhaps its grass becomes

a jungle

where the hoofs of those grazing before

press an old track,

fitting precisely around exposed roots

in cracked clay…

My dreams carry me,

sometimes through an entire day,

and while my forebears

don't carve my way,

they too reside

on this earth I continue to walk

where, in the crossing paths of clouds,

the images informing sleep

bring coyote trotting,

between us only the window

upon waking.

COME BACK

And who ever taught you

you weren't enough?

Taught you what about you

was ugly

or missing

or un-lady-like or

not-man-enough

or too sensitive

or crazy?

And when, dear one,

did you start believing them?

Because the fullness of you,

the whole spectrum of your Being,

is exactly what you are called here to be.

Shunning the calling,

you shut the door on your Self.

Come back,

your spark is needed.

IN THE LABYRINTH

A little lost

in the labyrinth..

Come,

I say, come.

The unpaved road you walk-

soft powder underfoot and bowl of sky-

was not given.

It belongs to you,,

Yours,

forever, yours,,

Hear what must be understood.

This separation you identify with,

that cracking glass,

you have let it define you..

Come forth.

Come forth,

with each step a prayer

and release.

The beating in your chest

is My rhythm.

No difference,

no difference

between.

STORM SESSIONS

.Storm sessions of the mind.

Sight of one we had walked with,

hand in hand,

suddenly contorts our face in revulsion.

Another, whose breath we shared,

becomes the reason we spin,

alone without sleep.

Yet another,

whose laughter once joined ours,

we now shake a finger at.

The rain gathers

the pressure drops

the seas rise…

Become the arch of rock

unquestioning of its strength,

joyous to receive the downpour

and crashing glacial blue waves

that wash and sculpt it

into a singular masterpiece-

AT THIS HOUR

Up with owl.

And out,

before fog drip and spider's web part ways.

Artemisia and oat still bow their heads,

in gratitude for a wet night,

while crows have yet to forfeit rule of the streets,

and continue strutting the sand.

Acorn woodpeckers parked high up their holey electrical pole

discuss boldly the day before them.

Gull wings through thick white,

otter cruises shore's edge.

At this hour, smiles arise between passers-by.

HAVING NOT KNOWN WANT

Having not known want.

Desire, yes.

Longing,

for year after early year.

But needs unmet,

definitely not,

except

when it came to the intangible.

For those essentials,

I dug

and scraped

howled out

climbed towards

cooked up

excised and wound-dressed

myself.

Skills built by me,

for me,

with generous allies coming and going,

allowing this wayward spirit

to be, finally, available

to the rest of life-

sharing inspiration

with the wild.

TEAR THEM ASUNDER

I am not the fantasy

in your head.

Not savior, not goddess, not whore.

This demon you will wrestle alone.

I'm neither answer nor mistake.

Take those cords you wrap yourself in

and cut them-

they've no use for tying up dreams.

That which you seek,

you already walk in the heart of.

And the blinders obscuring your knowing

require your own two bare hands—

Go,

tear them asunder.

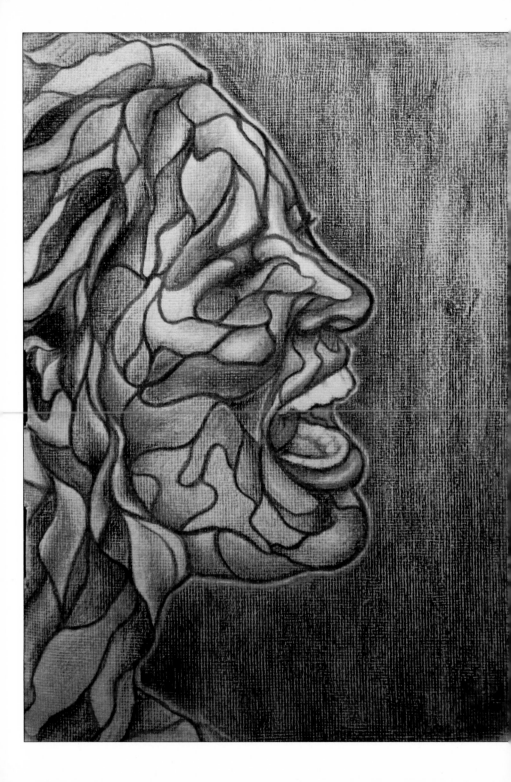

BETWEEN CEMETERY AND RESTING FIELD

Birds chatter in the walnut tree,

here,

between cemetery and resting field.

Butter yellow sunlight crosses

folds of canvas.

Mortared stones warm,

church bell rings.

The beagle's collar jingles

as he circles a man-

hand-knit brown wool sweater,

dark trousers,

rifle hanging from his shoulder-

slowly walking.

Today,

a hunt for rabbit and pheasant.

Through the open door,

a woman's voice rises in song.

CONVINCING STORYTELLER

Were I still to believe this tear

to be everything,

possibility would be lost.

Sorrow swallowing the world-

a familiar swimming channel.

Blind to the rainbows

in globes of salt water falling

from my own eyes-

Illusion makes a convincing storyteller.

Were I still to believe,

there'd be no seeing.

Perhaps, I am as much a fascination for the juncos

as they for me.

Laughter pushes streams down

pink cheeks

too-

And how it does bubble up.

BRING THE STORM

Invisible movements bring the storm.
Branches respond,
and limber green grasses.
Faces of hidden ones twitch,
their noses active to the shift;
they need not see,
they know.
Bring the dry in from approaching rain,
place that needing purification out
to wash
in sky rivers.
Small things, they come
and come and come and,
in release of their pleasure
space is created.
As, in endings, (for they come
and come and come and),
in their freeing make room for more.
Tides rise and fall,
rise and fall,
in me, in you..
honor the perfect imperfection-
We've always one another
to hold and
let go...

OPEN PALMS

I don't know where I'm going

but I know how to get there.

From you, I want

nothing.

My hands no longer carry that stone.

I walk on the wave

of what we shared and

I thank you.

A bird rests in my open palms now.

She takes spontaneous flight

and returns

beautifully unbidden.

Undiscovered story, footsteps yet to fall,

these are mine,

five toes by five toes,

inhale by exhale…

Goodbye meant losing everything

but my Self.

SILLY HUMANS

How scared we are of being
meaningless
unwanted,
rushing to make our accomplishments
known.
False identities choke us.
Silly humans.
These doings haven't anything to do
with our goodness.
They are nice
maybe,
or great
even,
perhaps amazing, delightful, honorable
and expressive of our innate beauty,
but essence is not
a woman's heart we must fight for,
or a man whose eye we must catch,
or the nodding approval of our father,
or the celebration,
at last,
of the person we are,
thrown by everyone that matters
(for better or worse),
because
-really-
the breath holding us to life
and back from death
already understands exactly
how powerful
loving and precious it is.
And we are that.

ECSTASY

Hair across face,

sheets spun,

sweat,

satisfaction.

Longing for other

traps more than passion,

destroy it and be

your best lover.

Hold Beloved's hand

by taking your own-

Ecstasy requires only One.

COULD BE

When the question comes,

What's wrong with you?

Could be,

Nothing at all.

THE UNINTERRUPTIBLE SONG

In the reaching comes the wobble,

and its music.

Beyond this silly dance is grace~

let us drink that silent nectar,

and leap,

without hesitation,

into the dive,

whorling slowly in

to where the cadence of current and pulse

are indistinguishable.

Doubts,

mosquitos of misdirection,

buzz our ears, yet

by learning to hear the uninterruptible song,

in time,

they will no longer swarm

as rhythm and spiral enfold us

in wedded movement.

I WON'T BE WAITING

Dedicated to someone who cares enough

to ask questions.

Let Nina Simone play,

while squared espresso cups

send steam up

to meet the wind.

I think I can waltz,

with myself and the mirror,

at least.

Crisp sheets beckon,

my fingers as good a lover

as any.

New mountains outside unfamiliar windows

call

and I, for one, can wait,

letting tension for satisfaction

build.

You'll come someday.

I've steep paths to climb with bold skies overhead.

Feel free to join me,

but make it interesting-

I keep a fast pace and

I won't be waiting.

WILD ONES

Wild ones come

in waking and sleep

blurring lines between worlds

Dream unfolds open-eyed

as those of night

visit through day,

pawing the same paths

with blazing eyes held,

or dropping close on whispered wing

taking advantage of a break

in the trees

The mystic bothers not

with real

unreal

One is inseparable

and messages reach the intended,

the veil only myth.

I RESIDE

I reside between fire and water-

air and earth, the circular cradle.

I am the mountain lion

bounding to the glass you stare through,

meeting your gaze to say, Yes,

do not doubt,

it is you I am here for.

After sleeping a century last night,

and meeting day with wet mud toes,

untied hair becomes extensions of the tree,

grass sprouts,

twisting wind brings nuthatches to overhead branches,

chattering as they swing around in a morning

when scents sound

of Spring.

THERE IS A WOMAN

There is a woman here.

She walks.

All day she walks.

Setting out on the same road

every morning

a small bag on her narrow back,

jeans

barely covering her bird bones,

Forward she moves,

bearing herself through

whatever pain that outweighs her pack

by a lifetime.

OUT OF SLEEP

Dappled shade drops from grand sycamores,

Woman on bicycle pedals in heels

down cobblestone,

Small boy lags behind mother,

winding between outdoor cafe tables,

dragging one finger along peaks of chair backs,

Sunlight stretches past church spire,

flooding quiet shadow with wakefulness.

Morning traffic-

parents carrying children to school

on two thin wheels.

A gathering of friends with cigarettes,

building stories through accumulating years,

drinks coffee before work.

Man with cello. Man running to catch time.

Woman coasts past, adjusting shawl,

ears filled with private music.

Two monks in beige robes,

crosses hidden in folds of cloth at their waists.

Diesel engines. Rattling bike frames.

Pigeons take flight

into pale cloudless sky.

Bordeaux brightens out of sleep.

MIND THE DELICATE ONES

Eight nimble legs stretch
across my face,
skitter quickly past,
beneath an unknown corner
of warm morning covers.
Shiny
Black
Fast
Poisonous
Repeated visitations
since birth
leaving me in the dark,
until now.
I am she.
Choosing the quiet places
to be master architect
of her own home.
Delicate by design
Agile
Solitary
Capable
Strong
Graceful
Her qualities welcome,
especially when facing fears
quick and poisonous,
though they bite only
when unseen,
and uncared for.
Mind the delicate ones,
their power remains hidden
until needed.

ALL THE TIME WE HAVE

In your arms,

the quaking of heart stops,

breath finds its river flow,

rolling belly settles in surrender,

and muscles tensed for action,

tired from constant readiness, dissolve

in ambient warmth.

In this shelter,

the ticking clock no longer sounds,

its meaning lost, forgotten.

Morning birdsong becomes

the vertical light becomes

the first star of black opening night.

Let us linger here forever…

Thankfully, Beloved,

that's all the time we have.

MEDICINE OF SILENCE

Were her voice

hushed

the medicine of Silence

would stop at the sand on which it breaks,

the drum of night unable to find its way

from heartbeat past her lips..

Our shore is one and the same,

the Ocean

our origin and return...

For the ears attuned

the music will be heard,

again and again

dancing bodies will join,,

The rugged journey along coastline and mountain ridge

not

for naught.

From formless to form

we are instrument.

Standing on peak and cliff,

we are moved.

BARE FEET TO BARE EARTH

Every morning, often at dawn, I step outside,

taking bare feet into empty pasture.

Connecting the circuit between sky and earth,

as surely we are meant to do,

blood finds a clearer rhythm.

And the birds at daybreak

speak eagerly.

I listen.

And pray.

And when worldly cares wet-cement my perspective,

the best offering I can sound

is only

thank you.

STONE

When family

is a broken sandcastle,

pick up a stone.

One, tides destroy,

as they must.

The other,

they sculpt.

Hold that stone, and kick

a wide arc of sand while diving

through salty arctic water,

and build whatever

wherever

whenever you wish,

knowing your creations

protect the royalty

of your own nature.

CLICHÉ

While contemplating the potential benefits

of becoming a drunken recluse

writing the nights into oblivion,

the dishes drip in the rack,

clothes agitate,

bills disappear from the list,

replies send.

Teeth even get flossed.

Pouring my pain into a tumbler

and drinking it down, only

to smash the glass into satisfying bits,

and repeat. The sound of those shards

crack through mind and all, really, I have to do

is run out and buy cheap booze

and glassware I'm not attached to.

WILDNESS RATTLED

from bed i smile to see

two complete handprints

low

on a wall of glass,

an invisible companion kneeling

at the altar

of treetop and sky

outside,

while watering in crisp daylight, and

wrapped in perfumed shawl of flowering ginger,

a pair of steller's jays hops close,

the depth of my thirst mirrored by theirs

wildness rattled,

within drought, by human flood.

the growing challenge

to regain elements vital

to thrive

THE LONG JOURNEY

When the trees reach their greenest,

that is when I will fly,

wings strong and broad for the long journey..

with feathers, iridescent,

reflecting sky,

tail tasting coolness of clouds,

eyes bright with the adventure

of following the setting sun, and

my heart singing the song

of every hour,

each tear and bubbling laugh,

that ever was

WHAT FILLS MIND

Flameless fire in golden grass-

Morning touches brightly

what rests before her.

Bowing down,

forehead and hands to dirt,

the weightlessness of surrender.

A yard above,

single-chant bird song

and short celebratory flights

between acacia and pine,

delight the winged and earthbound alike.

What fills mind

perfumes the sky.

WALK SLOWLY

Walk slowly into day-

rabbit is shy.

When the holding of mind releases,

held muscle follows..

With heart carried forward

the jig in each step synchs

in rising rhythm,,

This number may be for two

or twenty,

but always for one and

the grin on a single visage

captivates wonder.

And she deserves to be charmed.

IN UNISON

I can not tie my heart to yours.

Ties bind us both.

You will pass,

like seasons

or visions

or the magic of a night dream,

but know I'm here,

this moment,

giving without reservation

while

I belong to one

who never leaves

and

it is in that heart where you and I join.

Rest your eyes from searching-

I need no back door for exit

because,

in this,

walls illude

and presence

locks our free steps

in unison.

IN THE REACHING

If, in the reaching,

you fall,

you'll always be caught.

It just may hurt.

What of it?

Learning grabs you and

eventually

you'll find

what you seek isn't

out there,

so you'll reach inward

and falling into your Self

means

no end of soft landings.

ON FALLING…

falling isn't a problem,

impact is.

and, even more, the fear of it.

falling's nothing but uncontrolled flight-

we test our wings

our strength

our skill, the elements, and belief

in ourselves.

what, really, would we be

without falling?

and how much of the sky

would we miss

without reaching?

HICCUP

Had I fallen through

I'd be dead

which is fine- that day will come

when it comes

but!

As spirit leapt from body

and reinserted itself

in that hiccup of time and motion

I giggled

because here I was

back with existence

and dancing could continue...

SCULPTED

For those who left,

I now know,

I asked you to go,

And the rivers of tears,

the ocean of grief and sorrow,

my hand-written invitation

welcoming the fire.

Cleaved in two-

rock, split-

through those openings

water washed and sculpted

hollowed out and

slowly

re-formed this being,

whose heart burned

and broke

over and over and over,

tumbling and grating in wave

after wave,

until

breath narrowly returned

from a final shattering,

freeing a Self

whose unalterable joy

demanded release.

COYOTE APPROACHES

Coyote approaches

and, upon sensing me,

sits

gracefully,

slowly

stepping out his front paws

to lay down face to face.

Honor,

a swell, rolls through

in response to such a gift

from the wild.

I'd sweep the skies with bare hands

to bring stars down

to light your way,

weave the needles at my feet

to bring canyon waters to your lips..

but you have all that.

The best I can give is my presence,

gratitude,

a full heart,

and respect for big ears, bushy-furred tail,

and your taste for the unexpected.

WALK WITH ME

Walking the live growing edge,

Flames of experience lick heels~

In this divine purification,

Ash feeds Earth,

Smoke tendrils rise in prayer, skyward,

Heart's passion strengthens,

Love becomes boundless,

Devotion deep,

and the weight of gravity,

a welcomed morning blanket

holding us here, joyfully embodied.

By Grace,

Presence expands,

Spark resides...

Come walk with me,

be a light for One

and another-

the view is breathtaking,

the vital pulse ever danceable,

and the space to share,

Infinite.

STILLPOINT

There is a point

at which we stop looking out

for yes

for okay

for be mine,

when need dissolves,

yearning cuts loose, and

hope and expectation walk away.

While strength climbs in the window

and peace holds us close,

the hunt for validation ceases,

dulling the barb of acceptance..

With that, a new sun

around which all else turns,

offers light,

ever undiminished, reflecting

even in night through a softly eager moon,

an illuminated way.

DEPARTING FLIRTATION

With red-shouldered hawk

standing

on my roof

and an old sorrow

abandoning its stolen post,

the chickadees gather

beneath the eave,

one sneaking away to the window

to brush the glass

in departing flirtation.

GUARDIANS

Two white owls

dusted with beige,

perch in pine.

Upon revelation,

visual impact,

I wake with a cry.

From familiar swoop of tree limb,

one faces water, the other

toward opposite earth.

Keeping watch over the unseen,

with them I slept.

Escaped voice suspends forming tears,

a crash out of dream,

surprise vigil.

Guardians.

Cradled in mind,

held in slumber,

worlds animate with closed eyes.

MORNING'S YAWN

Ducks in the shallow end

of calm intertidal,

Suspended garlands of kelp

in watery scoop of sand,

High bumps of cloud~

Morning's yawn unwinds.

A man wrapped in navy terry cloth and slippers

walks the slope of driveway for the paper,

A woman lounging in robe reads on her deck,

Another, in nightgown and raincoat, head bowed, smokes her first

cigarette,

A third, barefoot, hops back homeward from the car,

whatever needed gathered in hand.

A feather drops from the sky

on the way home.

FAMILY

Without hummingbird's gravelly persistence,

red-shouldered hawk's cries

from bending cypress

would have spread

into broad-winged flight.

But I miss that

to turn

and find coyote beside me.

Announcing myself, he looks.

Iridescent ones flit through shadow.

Adjusting his snout,

and lowering his haunches,

he negotiates

whether to have a seat or trot away.

Hummingbirds scatter as he heads southward.

THE NEXT TIME

My slipping my hand into yours

may be the slyest action I take

before daybreak..

Dream being such effortless invitation.

Where were you

when stars draped the blue black sky

and outlined pine crowns pressed the horizon?

My breath need not search yours,

the balance of inhale

and release

requests no reminders.

The next time I catch your lips behind my ear,

I'll be listening to your invisible passing

with more than a smile.

RABBIT AT DAWN

Meeting rabbit at dawn,

her form nearly a shadow in gold grass,

voices of three owls cross overhead.

Bat descends swiftly from behind,

grazes ground,

flies sharply up past my cheek.

Rabbit hops closer, stands high on hind feet,

bringing a clear river of scent to her twitching nose and,

with offset ears, sits, scratches, and

washes herself.

Dark full-bodied mosquitoes harvest breakfast

from my backside.

Red-shouldered hawk cries dominantly

from the west,

lands on cypress crown.

Young coyote trots by.

A BRIGHT FLOOD OF NUTHATCHES

A bright flood of nuthatches alight on young oak,

thoughts lift,

walk impossible angles,

hang from the feeding branch.

Bugs and birds, marriage of prey and predator,

a beginning and end allowing more

to begin.

In savory pause,

a break in the sky carries them away…

FULL POSSESSION

In the growing up
Vision clears.
With the bite of attachment
through hunger and loss,
Gifts-
Sap and nectar and perfume,
the rooted water finding,
nourishment gathering,
earth holding..
Blessings
present themselves
in an upwell of golden hour light,
offering full possession
of that which blindness said
didn't exist-
A mighty, sweet
and inexhaustible
power..
Ignorance is a back turned to the east,
a mind believing sunrise
to be myth.
Turn around,
the sky blushes for you.

BRING US PAUSE

Were this all-

the mirage within which we play our games-

colored light on night's sleeve,

dew resting on lips of the rose,

cricket song the whole day through,

skin brushing skin,

hand on metal hand on stone,

red kettle steaming,

serpent trail through dust,

squash blossoms...

these would not bring us pause~

for in a single breath moves

Eternity

I LET THE WIND SWALLOW ME

While blinking with coyote

I let the wind swallow me.

Three egrets fly upriver,

my eyes sweep down

to the mouth

where sweet and salt swirl,

tongues of worlds finding pleasure

in their opposing movements.

SHADOW

Shadow?

Mask changer,

character after character

in the play-

not villains, though

the audience holds its breath

still

with each entrance- -

I believed the acting.

I could not name you,

too caught in shifting storylines

until

moving to the back of the theatre,

when the stage became a stage,

and you! I saw

you wear the same shoes

with every performance..

Shadow?

Lithe one,

Let's dance…

SITTING, AWAKE, THROUGH THE NIGHT

When the zeros line up

it's only a new day

and all things are possible

(spoken best, of course, with the head waggle of a native Hindi speaker)

and the blankness before you

the discomfort of the void-

in that dark place, magic is born

where what normally hides from the day can play~

let it beckon with crooked mischievous finger

and whisper its haunting melody..

times come when the path must disappear

beneath your feet

and sitting, awake, through the night

may be exactly what is best for spirit

to guide you

BY NATURE

I am, by nature, bobcat,

solitary

feline

heightened in sense.

Within spinning social circles, coyote

trots through to play,

and joyful hummingbird dives and hovers,

sipping nectar along the way.

In mind, spider

builds architectural masterpieces,

suspends silken threads and

swings me across great expanses.

Owl emerges come night,

gathering the unseen for informed

and skilled movements.

The rest of day,

I soar as hawk

high above rugged lands

carrying both fine detail and grand formations

in my vision,

while mountain lion looks out

from ridge top,

assessing what lays before her.

WHEN WE HAVEN'T ANY IDEA WHERE ELSE TO GO

If i can reach you when the darkness surrounds you,
if there's a light i'm able to shine
to give direction when orientation disappears,
i count myself lucky.
Offering only what i know
from all the time i've been lost in the night
and faced the depth of pain a heart feels when it seems likely
to crack in two,,
i hold out not my hand
but point the way to the hand i hold,
and, in its small way, this act
may be what it takes for you to save your own life
because
that's what we do for each other,
and while i haven't much to give
i do understand the lasting needs~
kind words and laughter- when they come-
love
compassion
silence and listening..
you are not alone, for that which moves my blood,
moves yours.
we are not so unalike, you and i.
Let us sit at the invisible table
and taste
this day's hot brew when the cold wind whips
and we haven't any idea where else to go

Deep thanks to all who helped get us here-
family, friends, inspiring strangers, and every swirling element.
Michelle, Rolf, Sally & Tad and the boys,
thank you.

Perry Annan Rose

To contact Perry Annan Rose for books, or adventurous writing projects:
rootedingracemedicineofword@gmail.com

Amanda Burkman

To contact Amanda Burkman for prints or original artwork:
rustiwillow@gmail.com

Published 2014
Second Printing 2016

It's a Wonderful Life, Again!

by Regina Kinney

It's a Wonderful Life, Again!

Dedication

This book is dedicated:

First, to God and His glory

My soul mate, Jim Kinney

My brother, Dell Stewart

My only niece, Michelle Barron

My godmother, Mom Bea Paris

My wonderful lifelong friend, Tim

My friends Pat and Terry Underwood (Terry died 1-19-2005)

All my staff and nursing care friends:

The Med hospital, the nurses, the doctors, the staff, the trauma unit, the bariatric unit, the fifth floor staff

The girls who used to work at Justinian's and our customers

To all hairstylists

I dedicate this book to the glory of God, my family, friends, neighbors and to everyone who prayed for me while I was laid up for eight months recovering from my accident.

May God continue to richly bless you.

Love,

Regina Kinney

Acknowledgments

A special thanks to Twila Slezak for typing and putting my manuscript on disc.

A special thanks to a "special woman," Julie Kirk, at CSN Books. Julie, I appreciate your kindness, compassion, love and all the long hours of dedication in making *It's a Wonderful Life, Again!* a miracle story of life.

A special thanks to our family doctor, Dr. Ehud Kamin. Because of his work, my brother Dell, my husband Jim and I are living a healthier lifestyle. We love you, our friend and doctor.

May this book touch your mind, body and soul as it did mine.

Table of Contents

Preface

Being obese is pure hell. Unless you have been obese, you will never understand the life overweight people lead. It is very hard. You begin blaming everyone around you for your eating instead of taking responsibility for yourself. It is never your own fault. You hate your body, you hate your life, and you do not like living inside this turmoil called "everyday life."

I dislike it when someone says to me, "You sure do have a pretty face. If only you could lose some weight." I cannot tell you how many tears I have shed over my big, fat self, wallowing in self-pity. I cannot tell you how many stares I receive from others, the laughter I hear behind my back as people talk and make fun of me. The saddest part of all is that the ridicule and the hurtful words come not just from strangers, but from friends and sometimes even family.

When you have been obese for most of your life, there is a little person inside your body who wants out—to be free, to be able to experience true joy, hope and inner peace.

No one will ever know how many times I have prayed to "just be normal," not fat and labeled "obese" by the world around me. I long to be able to get my arms around my soul mate, Jim; to give him a big bear hug.

I prayed for 40 years for God to send me someone special in my life. God answered my prayers and gave me Jim and the family I so desperately longed for. Today, I have children that love their mother and grandchildren who love their grandma...and I received it all from Jesus.

CHAPTER ONE

Looking Back on Life

Trapped in Prison

All my life I have had a weight problem, starting after I had my tonsils removed. Before that, my throat always hurt and I could not eat much because of the pain. There have been times in my life, as I think back, that I wish I had kept my tonsils. "Maybe I wouldn't be obese today," I would think. Yet I knew that I was only kidding myself.

Not being able to sleep was also a problem. Getting up at 2:00 or 3:00 in the morning to watch television while eating something like peanut butter and bread was normal for me. However, I would not just have one or two slices; I would eat almost the whole loaf of bread.

I was unhappy most of the time because of the "prison" my body had me in. I would get especially depressed if someone would tell me how beautiful I was, but then qualify it by adding, "...if you could only lose weight."

I was a hairdresser for almost 30 years. Due to my health problems, I had to go on disability at the age of 47. This was one of the hardest decisions I have ever had to make in my life. Needless to say, I cried and prayed about this life-changing decision, but knew I could not continue. I had missed so much work; each time I called in, it put extra work on the other girls in the shop. Yet they took on that extra load without ever complaining to me.

My daily schedule after going on disability was a lot slower. I thought time at home would give me a chance to take better care of myself. Then something happened that was out of my control.

The Day Life Changed

On Saturday June 5, 2004, I got out of bed at 5:00 a.m. and put my feet on the floor as usual. My right leg was hurting. Since my body weight put a great deal of strain on my legs and feet, I always waited a few minutes before getting up onto my feet. This time when I began to stand up, I found myself doing open-wide splits! Everything happened so fast! Before I knew it, I was on the floor in front of my bed.

The pain was so bad that my screaming woke my husband. Jim heard my screams but could not find me! He cried out, "Where are you? What's happened?"

I told him I was on the floor in front of our bed. We keep our room very dark, so when he got out of bed to help me, he accidentally fell on me!

I said, "Baby, I hope you can get up because I know I can't."

Being tangled up in the dark made getting up far easier said than done. When Jim was finally able to free himself and stand, he turned on the bedroom light and tried to help me get up. He took my right hand and tried to pull me to my feet, but the pain was horrible. I asked him to bring me a pillow for my head and then call 911 for help.

While we waited for the paramedics to come, I told Jim, "I don't know what kind of damage I have done to my hip and back." What I did know was that I was in severe pain and desperately wanted help.

Finally the ambulance arrived. My husband had told them on the phone that I was a really large lady and they would need extra help, so they came prepared.

I do not remember how many men they sent, but I was not even embarrassed about my obesity. Obviously, I was in extreme pain. I also knew by the way my legs had stretched out that there was going to be some damage down there.

It took a lot of men to get me on an orange tarp to move me from my room into the living room. They laid me on the floor while they checked my sugar and my blood pressure. Then they asked me what hospital to take me to. I told them, "Baptist East on Walnut Grove."

When they finally took me out of my house and to the ambulance on the orange tarp, I was scared and worried about whether the hospital would allow me in because I did not have insurance.

In the emergency room at Baptist East, all I remember was I desperately wanted something for the pain. However, they could not give me anything until they knew what was happening to me.

At around 3:00 in the afternoon I was told I would have to be transferred, by ambulance again, to the trauma unit at the Med. At that point, I knew I was in for a long haul, because they do not send you to the trauma unit unless you are very badly hurt.

Another ride, this time on a stretcher, was even worse than the first; the pain nearly killed me.

CHAPTER TWO

Two Long Months in the Trauma Unit

Arrival

When I arrived at the Med Trauma Unit, I just wanted to have a little relief from the awful pain. Again, however, I had to wait until they figured out what was wrong. I was put in Room 10 with the best male nurse, Roger; he tried everything he could to make me feel better.

I cannot tell you how long it was before my family and I finally understood what kind of damage had been done when I had fallen. The wait seemed endless.

The doctor finally told us that my pelvis was broken. With my weight at almost 500 pounds, they said that I would have to have surgery to put something called a Greenfield filter in my leg. After the surgery, I would be laid up for about six months before I could put any weight at all on my legs.

They tried to insert the filter without putting me to sleep, but I could not stand the position in which they had to put me in order to do the procedure.

Under the Knife

The next step was to schedule surgery. That was scary because in my family we have a history of problems being put to sleep. My brother, Dell, had problems being put sleep when he had surgery, and even worse, my great-grandmother had died from being put to sleep before surgery. Thankfully though, I handled the general anesthesia just fine and went to sleep without any problems.

The surgeon inserted Greenfield filters into each leg in order to keep me from having blood clots while I was on extended bed rest. However, one of the filters moved from my leg into my pulmonary artery in my lung. The doctor told me that had never happened before.

While I was in surgery, the surgeon discovered that I had been born with two vena cava veins. The doctor explained this to me and said it was rare, though not completely unheard of.

The morning after the surgery my husband and brother came to see me. Jim asked, "Why is your mouth drawn on the left side?" I told him I could not move my left arm nor my hand either. I knew then that I had had a stroke, and my doctors needed to discover the cause.

Starting Over

We soon found out that the stroke had occurred because I had been born with a hole in my heart, and I was not getting proper blood flow from my brain. I have had migraine headaches since I was 13 years old and was 48 years old when this defect was discovered!

I was told I would have to have therapy to recover from the stroke. I had to perform therapeutic exercises on my left arm and hand, and learn to eat and smile again.

Therapy moved slowly. I kept my left arm on two wedges and had to make sure I left my fingers out so they would not lock up. Needless to say, I could not sleep and could not eat; I did not even want to try.

One day, one of the good-looking doctors came by my room; he did not know I was moving my left arm and hand, so he came in and asked me to smile for him. I squeezed his hand and stuck out my tongue and we just laughed.

Patching a Broken Heart

It seemed an endless wait before we found a doctor that could fix the hole in my heart. Finally, we learned of a doctor who did this type of surgery, mostly on children. This doctor told me that because of my weight he did not know if my heart could survive the procedure, but we had to do something. He scheduled me for surgery and I had to be transferred over to the surgical hospital that was somehow connected to the Med.

Before they laid me on the table, the doctor explained that I could die from this procedure. Still I was not worried; I was in God's hands and I knew He would take care of me.

I am happy to report the surgery was a success, and I no longer have migraine headaches!

The Daily Grind

So many things happened while I was in the trauma unit that I was not able to have a lot of company. There were many times when I was alone, with no one to talk to; so I talked to God out loud, telling Him, "I can't handle this; please help me to understand and get through this day."

Every time I did this, He always helped me.

I know if it had not been for my family, friends, church family and loved ones sending up prayers for me, I would not be where I am today.

My dear husband came every morning to make sure I got fed what little breakfast I could eat. I thank God for my soul mate, Jim!

I always looked forward to my visits from my brother, Dell, and his girlfriend, Peggy. They would come later at night, which was the hardest time for me.

It seemed like every time I turned around a nurse, doctor or someone else needed to do blood work. I got to the point that I hated to see anyone with a needle! Sometimes I had to get stuck three, four, even up to seven times before they could get any blood. One time they needed blood from my artery; it hurt so bad I said a word that I hate to hear! Another time they had to give me liquid potassium through my vein. There was so much pain from the blood work and blood gases!

Good Days and Bad Days

I had days when I was negative about everything. On those days, I prayed a lot, cried a lot, and if it had not been for my lack of appetite, I would have eaten as much as possible. I was glad on these days that I could not eat.

There were days when all I wanted was water and sometimes I could not even stand that. I remember one day the doctor told me, "Mrs. Kinney, you are going to have to eat. You are becoming malnourished." That was certainly hard to understand for someone my size!

The nurses were constantly calling the manufacturing company to work on my crazy bed. It threatened to drive the nurses and me crazy! One day I was trying to sit on the bed to let my feet down when all of a sudden, I ended up on the floor. Jim was in the room with me and tried to keep me from falling, but it seemed to happen in the blink of an eye. My nurse, Martha, said, "Regina, you scared all of us."

The next thing I knew there were about ten people in my room. Everyone was trying to figure out a way to get me off the floor and back into the bed. They struggled to get me onto a transport board. They were hurting me, but I knew they could not help it; the next thing I know they had lifted me back onto the bed. They all exclaimed, "Please don't try that again!" I was not about to! Once it was all over we all had a good laugh.

After I had my stroke, it took at least six people to give me a bath. Talk about giving up modesty! I had to learn to put laughter into my bath time because it was often two or three men and women who would give me a bath. Sometimes I used so much crazy talk that the men would walk off and find someone else to help with my bath.

Those who know me realize that crazy talk is just part of my personality. We who are obese have to have some kind of craziness in our lives or we could not live with ourselves!

The Worst Day

One morning Pastor Larry Bagby and his driver, Twila, came for a visit. When they got ready to leave, Jim and Dell followed them out the door and I heard Jim ask Larry to remember our friends Benny and Mary Welch in prayer. I thought to myself, "What's that about?" but I said nothing at the time.

A few nights later while I was on the phone with Dell, I said something about calling Benny to see how he and Mary were doing because I had not heard or talked to either of them in a while. I knew something was not right so I asked him to tell me what was going on. He hesitated but I kept right on asking until he finally told me that Mary had been in the hospital at Baptist East for three weeks. She had had a heart attack. Benny had given her CPR but at this time she was on full life support because everything had shut down and she was brain dead.

Dell said the reason he had not told me was that I had been through so much everyone was afraid this would set me back. It certainly was a shock! I knew they had done what they had felt was best for me. I remember hanging up the phone crying and praying for Mary and Benny. I know what the power of prayer can do.

Thankfully, Mary is still alive and doing as well as possible.

Small Miracles

One day I called my friend, Pat Underwood. It just so happened that she was at the hospital that day with her mother, Francis Brown. Francis was in surgery; they were removing a brain tumor. Pat and I talked for a few minutes. I told her that when I hung up, I would pray for her. I told Pat to be sure to call me when she knew anything.

When I got off the phone, I cried my heart out and then I prayed for Francis to make it through the surgery.

Later Pat called to tell me her mother had made it through the surgery, though she would have to have some therapy when she recovered.

One weekend my husband and our cousin, Gary Lewis, came to see me, on a day my bed was acting crazy again.

The nurses called the manufacturing company to come work on my bed. While he was working, the technician asked, "Did you know your bed can be converted into a chair?" Of course I had not known that! I had been in that bed for all that time, and this was the first time anyone had said it could go into a sitting position.

The technician asked me if I would like him to show me how to convert the bed; I told him yes. However, when he tilted the bed, I starting crying. He asked me, "What's wrong, honey?" I had gotten so dizzy that I felt like I was going to faint. So he stopped for a second and told me that it was natural that I get a little dizzy because I had been lying there for so long.

After a few minutes he asked, "Are you ready to try again?" I was; this time he got me into a sitting position.

It may not sound like much to you, but to me it was wonderful!

He let me sit up for a few minutes while he told me how to get the bed back down.

After this, different nurses would occasionally set the bed for me. Some did not know how...that was O.K. too.

The Med Trauma Unit

The Med is a life-saving trauma unit where the doctors, nurses and specialists of all kinds treat patients with many emergency needs. They face some very tough situations and decisions. It is a very busy, complicated place where the staff is stressed by long hours and constant life-saving decisions.

If you have never been in a trauma unit you would be amazed at what can go on in just a minute, let alone one day! There is always someone being flown in by helicopter at all times of the day and night. Some of my nights were spent praying for whoever was in the helicopter, asking that God would spare the life and help their families deal with their trauma.

There was always so much going on; people of all kinds, helping this one or that one. Each life was just as important as the next life. If you really need to appreciate a healthy life, go visit a trauma unit. You will thank God for all He has given you. You will realize how precious life can be and how it can be taken away in a moment.

By the Grace of God

My days in the Med were long, painful and hard for me, my husband, Jim, and my brother, Dell. I thank God for all the prayers I received from family, friends, loved ones—especially Twila and Pastor Larry Bagby. Many prayer requests also went out to different churches all over the city.

The only reason I was able to do what had to be done was because God sustained my health. I know He loves me; He sent me to the right places to get me back on my feet. However, all this took time.

There were many days I wanted to just get up and try to walk. I even imagined walking over and getting myself something to drink. I never gave up hope in my heart. I knew I would walk again. This is what kept me going on day after day. Unless you have been in a similar situation, you will never know how hard this was.

Many people asked me, "How did you stay in bed that long?"

I did it by the grace of God.

CHAPTER THREE

The People Behind the Scenes

The Chaplains at the Med

My preacher, Larry Bagby, and his driver, my friend, Twila Slezak, would come visit me when they were able. Larry and Twila were a blessing to me, as were my husband and my brother. Larry would call and pray for me on the phone; anytime I needed a prayer I would call him and he would pray.

There were chaplains in the Med; one of them was Chaplain Dale Bilbrey, a friend of my pastor. Larry asked the chaplain to come see me; he came by every chance he got. We talked about life in general, and about me being moved all over the hospital and him always finding me no matter where they had moved me. He prayed some beautiful prayers for me and brought me gospel tapes.

In addition, there was Chaplain Susan. She would also manage to find wherever they had moved me.

One day my husband and brother were eating in the cafeteria and my brother recognized a lady named Susan who had been in his wedding years ago. She came over to speak to Dell, asking him what he was doing at the Med. He told her about everything I had been through. She found out what room I was in and from then on she would come see me as well. Thank you, Chaplain Susan!

I loved my chaplains at the Med.

Diet Sprite and White Crackers

A young lady came into the trauma unit on drugs, having a lot of problems. One night she was giving our nurse a lot of trouble, so I asked the nurse if she could come in my room and visit with me. The nurse asked her and she came in. We talked for a while; she told me she had two children.

This girl was a beautiful young lady. I was old enough to be her mother; it about broke my heart to see her in such pain. She said her stomach was hurting. I let her have a Diet Sprite and some white crackers, and then she went back to her room. She was waiting for a visit from her dad; I could tell she loved her daddy.

I was on the phone with my friend, Jamie, when someone knocked on my door. I told Jamie I would call her back. It was the young lady and her dad. She had brought him to meet me, which made me feel great.

She asked me if she could get another Diet Sprite; of course I agreed. Her dad tried to pay me for the drink, but I said, "Don't even think about it. Put your wallet back in your pocket." They took her drink and went back to her room.

The next morning before breakfast she stopped in for a minute; I told her to come back around 9:00 so I could introduce her to my husband and my brother. She came over and kissed me on the cheek and left. She did not know, but after she left my room I cried for her. My heart hurt for her and her children.

At 9:00 she came back and met my family. Then the nurses came and got her for something; I never knew what. It was not long after this I got moved again.

My heart still hurts for her and her dad and family. I cry whenever I think of her. This young lady touched my heart; I will never forget her. Wherever this young lady is, I hope she knows I love her and pray she is living a different life, a better life with even more love than she had when I first met her.

I Thought I Had It Bad

I often could not sleep because of the pain. Every night I would play the gospel tapes Chaplain Dale had brought to relax me and to drown out the noise of the helicopters landing. One weekend I counted seven helicopters landing on top of the building! When this happened I remembered that even though I had problems there was always someone else in bad shape, maybe even worse than myself.

At one point there was a man in the room across the hall from me who had been shot. I could hear the family crying and talking about this surgery or that problem. My heart felt so sorry for his family, and for others who were dealing with a dying child, or a sick daughter or son, or mother, father, grandmother, grandfather, aunt, uncle, cousin or friend—whoever it may be—not knowing if they would make it through surgery or whatever they were going through at that time.

Cherished Visitors

I have always been one to wait on others. I cannot tell you how many times I wanted to get out of that bed and just be able to wait on myself! Imagine being laid up for almost two months, unable to bathe yourself, shave your own legs, wash your own hair, go to the bathroom in private! Can you imagine how hard it is to have to have someone help you with these things, not just every now and then, but constantly, for two months? I had times of depression that were so deep I just wanted to give up.

Thank God for my telephone! I called my godmother, Mom Bea and my friends, Jamie and Pat. We loved to talk! I even caught myself talking to myself—sometimes I answered too!

In the trauma unit, you were only allowed two visitors at a time. It was hard not having many visitors except for my husband and Dell, and occasionally Dell's girlfriend, Peggy. When I had company I cherished them.

One day, in walked my godmother, Bea Paris, and her family: Greg, Vicky and Sarah Evans. Vicky had made me a fruit basket, but more important than anything she had brought my precious Mom Bea and her family to see me. That is one day I will never forget, and I know Mom Bea won't either.

A couple of my customers and dear friends, Terry and Pat Underwood, came to see me in one of the trauma units. They brought me an arrangement of flowers that Terry had made; I had not known he was that talented! They stayed for a little while. We laughed together as we always do, and of course Terry had to tell a joke or two. He was always telling me a joke.

When Terry got his hair cut or beard trimmed at the shop, many of the customers thought he was my brother, and I did love him like a brother. Whenever Terry spent time with his best friend, Rick Provow, Pat would visit us so that the men could have time together. She, Jim and I would play games.

Sadly, Terry is not with us anymore. He passed on January 19, 2005, before I got home from my ordeal. As I was still in the hospital, I was not able to attend his funeral. That has been very hard to accept.

Another friend, Jamie Brown, came to visit me. I was on the fifth floor at the time, finally in a regular room. She brought me flowers and an angel. We visited briefly; I was very glad she had made the effort to come to see me. Jamie and her husband Robert Brown prayed for me every day and prayer meant more to me than any visit, even though I did enjoy my visits!

Ups and Downs

Of course that is not to say that anyone who did visit me was not also praying. I know they were. There were so many days I felt God's presence in my room; I knew He was there with me. It was wonderful! I never lost my hope and joy; without them I never could have made it. Up to this point, I had never truly understood pain and suffering, not just from the accident but from the loss of living. I wanted my life back so badly sometimes I could almost taste it.

One day I remember thinking about going over to the sink and fixing myself a diet drink and something to snack on, but of course I realized I was still in bed. I had never thought I would see the day when I did not want food as much as I wanted out of that crazy bed! I wanted so badly to just put my feet on the floor.

Sometimes I would make myself so upset over stupid things. When you have only time on your hands with nothing to do but lay there, it can be horrible one minute, and not so bad the next.

Other times, my heart would hurt for my friends. One day, Larry Bagby called to tell me that Twila's daddy had been sick for a while. Later, he called to let me know that her father had died and she was going home to Nebraska for a while. It seemed like I was always getting some sort of news—sometimes bad, sometimes good.

Favorite Nurses

A few of my nurses stand out in my mind. One nurse, I cannot recall her name, was a big girl. She was getting ready to have gastric-bypass surgery to lose weight. We hit it off really well. She took the time to let me know that she understood about my weight, even though she was not nearly as overweight as I was. Then I got moved again and was never able to hear the results of her surgery. She was a sweetheart.

A male nurse came into my room one day, shut the door and told me about his drug problem. Because he understood about the abuse of drugs, he could understand the abuse I had for food. He stayed in my room for a long time. We talked, we laughed, we cried together, and we hugged and we kissed each other on the cheeks. He probably could have gotten into serious trouble had they known what he was telling me, but he helped me and I helped him and that is all that mattered in the end.

There were so many nurses and doctors—male and female—who helped me more than they will ever know.

Nurse Vicki learned to give me my bath alone, which was an amazing blessing. Every day she made sure I got everything I needed. She hung all my cards on the blinds in my trauma room.

Vicki was one of my favorite nurses. She went out of her way to help. I could call on her whenever I wanted and she always made it a point to come as soon as she could.

I had my husband bring our wedding picture to the hospital so everyone could see that I had not always looked as bad as I did now. Every now and then, I would make a comment about how bad I looked, and every time someone would tell me that I did not look that bad. I guess considering all that I went through I could have looked worse. My wedding picture got looked at a lot because I was always telling someone to look at it; we clean up well.

CHAPTER FOUR

Moving On

Last Day at the Med

On August 10, 2004, I got up early, ate breakfast, and talked to a few friends: Mom Bea, Jamie Brown, Pat Underwood and Dell. It was my last day at the Regional Medical Center at Memphis (the "Med"). I was leaving, not for home but to the healthcare facility in Jackson, Tennessee.

This was a hard move because I knew I would be away from my home, friends, family and loved ones.

My pastor called. He wanted to make sure he got to the hospital with Twila in time to see me one more time before I left Memphis.

Jim finished packing up the things that I needed for Jackson and we waited for the ambulance and the paramedics to show up.

Larry and Twila made it to my room just a few minutes before the paramedics. They stayed a few minutes to tell me goodbye and to pray as always.

I took four pain pills for this ride to Jackson; they were not sure how much pain I would be in. I said my goodbyes and thanks.

The paramedics brought the stretcher, got me on it, and I was ready to go. Jim took my things out to my red truck and met the ambulance out front so he could follow behind them.

After the paramedics loaded me in, they made sure to make me as comfortable as they could. The driver was kind and loved to talk. The paramedic who road in the back with me was named Michelle, she was kind and sweet. We all talked almost all the way, and before I knew it we were nearly there.

They called the Jackson Fire Department to get directions, but we still got lost. They had to call one more time and stop at a service station as well.

My husband went to the restroom at the service station and when he came out he went one way and we went another. I knew this because I did not see my red truck behind the ambulance. We went on and finally found the place; thankfully, so did my husband.

It was so good to finally be out of the Med and on to where I was going to get my therapy, get back up on my feet and then back to my life again.

First Day at the Healthcare Facility

After we finally arrived, the paramedic went in to make sure we were at the right place. The paramedics had told the Jackson Fire Department they needed help, but they did not help. Instead there were several employees who came out to help get me out of the ambulance. Each person that worked at the healthcare facility introduced themselves and they all made me feel like I was at the right place. They took me into my room, number 106, and I continued meeting different certified nursing assistants (CNA) and the heads of different departments. My husband then started to bring my things out of the truck. He unpacked my clothes, shoes and socks and put them on the shelves and in the drawers.

Jim stayed for a while so he could rest a little. He had gotten up early and was getting tired, so I eventually told him it was O.K. for him to leave, that I would be fine. I knew he still had the hour and a half ride home. We said our goodbyes; I would see him again the next weekend.

After he left, I met a few more people, including a man named Bill. The staff had told me to be aware of him; he was O.K., just lonely.

The rest of the day was fine. I had made up my mind to just make do with the best of all this.

Moving Up to a Wheelchair

On Friday, October 10, 2004, my two therapists decided to see if they could get me up with the lift and harness. They were successful. They helped me put on a pair of red pants and red shirt—the first time I was able to wear clothes! They took me in my wheelchair through the hallways; someone went and got a camera and took my picture with my friend, Laura, and Ronnie, the floor-man, then they brought me back to my room and put me back into bed.

It was so good to get up for a little bit! Of course I had to show everyone my picture.

More Good Days and Bad Days

Our eighth wedding anniversary was on October 13th, 2004. My sweet husband and his daughter, Carole, came to spend a little time with me to celebrate. They had made an orange dream sickle cake and Jim had brought me flowers.

We decided that when my friend, Laura, came in the morning to visit, we would cut the cake. Unfortunately, Laura fell and had to go back to her room to get checked out to make sure she was O.K. We went ahead and cut the cake without her. I ate a piece; it was good! Jim and Carole also ate a piece, and we sent the rest to the kitchen. We visited a little while, then Jim and Carole left and I went to bed.

After supper, I got the cake and brought it back to my room. I was happy to be able to share some with my friend, Thelma, her daughter Tiffany, a few other friends and some of the employees.

It was a good anniversary.

Not many days later, Jim called to tell me that Dell had gone to the doctor for his yearly checkup and the doctor had sent him for more tests. The tests revealed a tumor on Dell's colon; it was cancerous.

Dell had to have surgery to remove the tumor and later on he would have to have some treatments. This was hard on me and Dell as we were very close. All we could do was talk on the phone every day and pray for each other. I thank God for Jim and our cousin, Gary Lewis, who did everything they could for Dell while we were apart.

A filling came out of my tooth and began to drive me crazy with pain. One morning I could not even do my therapy. I asked the social worker, Dorothy, if there was any way to get a dentist to check my tooth. She told me the dentist only came twice a year, so I had to suffer it out. It kept me up for a few days. One of the nurses ordered me a special toothpaste and it helped somewhat.

Painful Trip to Memphis

I had a doctor's appointment on Monday, October 18, 2004, at the Med in Memphis to see how I was progressing after my stroke.

I got up early, ate breakfast in my wheelchair, got back in bed and waited for them to come. I ended up eating lunch in bed. When the ambulance finally arrived, they had not brought the stretcher that would hold my weight, so they had to send for another stretcher. As a result, we were leaving Jackson about the time I was supposed to be in Memphis.

When we arrived late, they were upset. They said they had already called Jackson looking for us. I was left on the stretcher in an "up" position because there was no one to help them put the stretcher down closer to the floor. I began to hurt badly. One of the black nurses in the office heard me crying and said she would get the doctor in as soon as she could. Two doctors came in and checked me out. They checked my reflexes, my left side, my right side and my left eye which had been affected by the stroke. My eye stayed numb all the time.

The paramedics had been told the appointment would take an hour, so they had gone to get something for lunch. However, the appointment only took 20 minutes. By the time they came back, I was in tremendous pain, though it was not their fault.

We headed back to Jackson; I was still in pain. The paramedics made me as comfortable as they could. We talked about how upset the Med staff had been when we were late, but it was just a misunderstanding. I remember passing an offramp that was near my house wishing I were home.

We finally got back to Jackson; when they wheeled me in it was almost 8:00 at night. A few of my friends, and even little Laura, who goes to bed early, were waiting for me. They were getting a bit worried. Whey they found out I was O.K., just in pain, they all went to bed.

The paramedics got me into bed. Someone brought me my supper and told me to call my husband who had called earlier. I stopped eating and called him back. Then I tried to go to sleep, but could not get comfortable enough, so I put on my gospel tape and eventually I fell off to sleep.

Walking Again!

In November, 2004, all my prayers were answered, as well as those of my entire family—my friends; my pastor and church friends; my godmother, Mom Bea; friends from different churches—everyone who had been praying and keeping the hope and faith that I would walk again.

I had been keeping a record of my therapy and my attempts to walk. There were days when I was in severe pain; on those days my therapist would skip my therapy. They told me that during those times of severe pain it would not help me to push myself.

At first there were more days that I had to push or I would have been lazy, and that is not me at all. I am usually a good go-getter, but this pain sometimes got my go-getter.

On Tuesday, November 9, 2004, I walked about 70 feet and only stopped once. I also stayed up out of bed from 2:30 to 3:30 in the afternoon. That may not seem like much, but after staying in bed for a little over five months, it was hard to do because I was in pain. As everyone knows, however, "No pain, no gain."

More Firsts

After many months I finally got in the shower for the first time since my accident. Talk about something feeling good! I got to wash my own hair and my own body. Bonnie was in the shower with me to help me get in and wash. After all, I had lost my modesty long before.

I enjoyed the shower so much; I looked forward to it again. It sure beats a bath and a shower in bed. If you have never had a bath in bed, count your lucky stars!

Not many days later I went to my first activity. I was feeling a bit better—I had been improving a little each day—so I went to the dining room to help make pumpkin pies. Of all things to make, wouldn't you know we would be making something I do not like at all!

I sat at a table with three other ladies. Shirley came to each table and let each one of us add an ingredient. We helped mix the batter up, then she poured it into pie crusts and took each one to the kitchen refrigerator.

I cannot recall how many pies we made. They ate them later which did not hurt my feelings, since I do not care for them anyway. I love to bake; it made me feel like I was in my own kitchen again.

CHAPTER FIVE

Enduring the Season

Giving Thanks

My husband and my brother came to visit me on Thanksgiving Day. We went to the dining room for lunch and ate at Tim's table. They had tablecloths on the tables for the occasion. We ate turkey, dressing, potato salad, English peas, macaroni and cheese, cranberry sauce, rolls and dessert (peach cobbler). It was all very good.

It was a good day to be very thankful. I was able to have my family with me—it was the last visit I would have with Dell. He could not make any more trips to Jackson, so I would not see him again until I left the healthcare facility and went home. It was hard to see them go, knowing I would not see Dell for a long time. I was so thankful for that time with him.

The weekend after Thanksgiving was quiet. I got up, ate breakfast in my wheelchair, then later went to the dining room for lunch. After I walked a little, I was tired and just watched TV While I was watching, Jim called and told me that Pat Underwood's mother, Francis Brown, had died. She had been in the hospital for awhile, when I was in the

Med. She had had a brain tumor removed. It had come back and she had not been doing well.

Even though this was expected, it was so hard to be away from home, especially when there was a death, knowing I could not be there for the funeral and for my friend. It was hard and it hurt. Still, I was thankful for the years Francis had lived.

One December morning, I ate my breakfast in my wheelchair as usual then walked my hallway. I only sat down once, and then laid down until lunchtime. Afterwards, Tim and a few friends were sitting out in the hall talking and it came over the intercom for me to pick up on line one.

Someone wheeled me over to the phone. It was my disability lawyer. He had called to tell me that my disability had finally been approved and that my husband should begin looking for it in the mail.

We talked for about 15 minutes. He wanted to see how I was doing. I told him about my stay here, my friends and how my walking was improving. Jim and I were so glad God was providing for us!

Christmas Cheer

Monday mornings were always noisy after being so quiet on the weekends. One Monday morning in December I did my usual morning routine and then after lunch I went to activity, where Shirley passed out boxes of Christmas cards. She told us to pick out two cards each, and if we were not able to write them she would help us. I wrote out and addressed one to my husband and one to my brother.

I began getting Christmas cards in the mail and we put them on my room door so everyone could see them. We even had a Christmas decoration on our door. Mine was an angel.

Another activity time in December was making fudge. Shirley had all the ingredients on a cart. She came to each table and let each one of us at the table add an ingredient. This really made me feel like Christmas was near. I always tried to make fudge, but mine never turned out as good as my mother's.

Once we finished Shirley said we would get to eat it later, but I never did. I am not sure where I was when it was served, but making it was fun!

One Monday afternoon Shirley, my friends and I made and decorated Christmas cookies. I had not baked cookies for years. Laura, Joyce and I cut out Christmas trees and bells and decorated them. One lady we all called "Honey" came over to me, so I asked her if she wanted one of the cookies. She started eating them about as fast as I could get them decorated. It did not matter how they looked or whether they had chocolate, white or green icing, she ate them. We all enjoyed this very much. It was fun.

Time to Celebrate

My husband, Jim, was supposed to play Santa for us at our Christmas party, but instead he was at home because of the snow and ice on the roads. I told him not to even try and come. It was too dangerous.

My friend, Tim and I went together to the party. We sat by the Christmas tree near the table that held the punch. We wanted to look at the beautiful tree. The staff had put lots of presents under the tree for everyone. They served us food and passed out gifts while we ate. We had punch, chips and dip, pizza and all kinds of desserts.

Everyone was talking at the same time. I watched different friends open their gifts. It was fun seeing how excited this one and that one got about his or her gift. Tim got a pair of pajamas, and I got a cross necklace that my husband had left me the last weekend he had visited me.

Someone had donated money to give each of us a thermal blanket. When my friend Charles got his, he did not like it, so he asked me if I had gotten mine yet. He wanted to know if I would exchange with him. When I got mine, which was a fall-colored design, we exchanged. I really liked his better, so we were both happy. The Christmas party was enjoyed by all of us; the staff made it a fun and special day.

On the morning of Christmas Eve, I got up and ate breakfast in my wheelchair. I went for a walk with Laura at 10:30 and only sat down once. I was able to use my potty chair for the first time—believe me, it sure beats being on the bedpan.

At 2:00 someone read, "Twas the Night Before Christmas" to us for our activity. After supper I spent time with my friends as always; it was a good day.

Christmas morning I woke up early at 5:30 a.m., and I could not go back to sleep. Everyone was beginning to get up and get ready for the day. I could hear different people in the hall talking, so I got up in my wheelchair and waited on breakfast in my room.

I walked half of the hall and waited for my friend, Tim. He and I went to the dining room together for lunch. It was a hard Christmas; it was the first time in my 48 years to be away from my family and loved ones. It was difficult, but we all made the best of a hard situation.

More Holiday Fun

Nita, my CNA, was very busy the Sunday morning after Christmas so I watched several church services. I ate lunch in my wheelchair until she came to give me my bath. Then Jim and Gary came to visit. Gary and my other family members waited for me in the hallway, and I surprised them when I walked out of my room. The first one I saw was my daughter, Penny. She almost had a fit seeing her mama walk. Then I saw my son-in-law, Robin, and my grand-daughters, Nichole, Lyne and Jamie. There were too many of us to stay in my room or in the hall, so we all went to the dining room for the rest of our visit. It was so good to see my kids!

The next day I got up early again and ate breakfast. Laura came to walk with me. I ate lunch in my wheelchair, watched TV and visited with my friends. In the afternoon I went to activity. Since it was close to the end of the month, we celebrated anyone who had had a birthday in December. It was something they did every month. We had birthday cake and I ate some even though I was not supposed to.

I got up late on New Year's Eve. It was 10:00 so I waited in my room for lunch. I went on a short walk alone and went to the dining room for lunch. Then with Nita, I walked the hall and only stopped once.

George helped me get in bed at 3:15, then I ate supper in my wheelchair and Tim and I watched TV with other friends. New Year's Eve was lonely; there was not much going on. They had an early New Year's Eve party, but I have never been one for going to New Year's Eve parties.

New Year's Day arrived, ringing in a new year with me still waiting for it to be time to return home. I was improving somewhat, though still having pain, but as I keep saying, "No pain, no gain."

A few days later I went to Bible study, which I always enjoyed—sometimes we would sing. I went back to my room to use my potty chair which was gradually getting a little easier. At activity time, Shirley made donut holes out of canned biscuits. She also made glaze icing. I ate three donuts and three donut holes and I believe this was one of my favorite treats ever. I have had donut holes before but these were the best. They were still hot and good with our milk. When I went back to my room I knew I needed to walk after eating those donuts, so I walked from 7:00 to 7:30.

Sad Times

On January 10, 2005, I slept until 11:30. For some reason I had a feeling something was wrong. I was lying down when my husband called around 4:00. He had called to tell me that my daddy was in the hospital.

After the usual evening routine, my brother called at 9:15. We talked for awhile and he said that Daddy was not doing well.

A few days later Jim and my cousin, Gary, visited. It was Gary's birthday. We had let the kitchen staff know they were going to be eating with me. We enjoyed the day.

Unfortunately, later that night Tim had a headache and was not feeling well. Joyce sat out in the hall with me. She liked to visit with me. I always gave her soda and some kind of food. She loved peanut butter and crackers. In fact, we all loved our peanut butter and crackers.

On Wednesday, January 19, 2005, I got up and went to exercise class at 10:30. Shirley helped me put my weights on my legs so I could do the leg exercises. Then she helped me put them on my arms to do those exercises.

My husband called to let me know that my customer, Terry Underwood, who had been sick and in and out of the hospital, had died that morning. This was a shock! He and his wife, Pat, also a customer, were dear friends. She had not yet gotten over the loss of her dear mother and had now lost her husband.

I could not sleep. I could only wonder how Pat going to make it through another death this close to her mother's at a time when she needed her husband the most. Then I thought about being stuck here in this bed, not able to go to the funeral and be there for Pat. It hurt my heart so much. I finally put on my gospel tape and fell asleep.

Special Treats

One day during activity class at 2:00 we ate my Aunt Kaky's coconut cake. Shirley cut it so everyone had a piece, and she also made something called a peach smoothie. I gave mine to Tim; I did not care for it. Still, we all enjoyed the time we spent eating and talking a little. Eventually I had to go back to my room as my leg was really hurting me again.

Later in the week after Bible Study one day, Shirley let me come over to the feeding table to help make peanut butter and jelly sandwiches for the dining room. I made peanut butter with grape, strawberry, apple and apple butter jelly. We had milk to drink. What would a peanut butter and jelly sandwich be without milk?

One Sunday morning I was up at 7:15. I sat on the side of the bed and ate my breakfast, and then Jim and Gary came. We went to the dining room for lunch again. After they left, I rested until Tim came and asked if I was going to go to church. I got up and went to the service from 3:30 until 4:30. We enjoyed George, Stephanie and some of the congregation of their church. I then ate my supper on the side of the bed. I walked the hall a lot that night. Tim kept a watchful eye on me, making sure that I was alright.

Medical Procedures

The night before my next doctor's appointment, Tim and I were talking and George was there, so we decided to get him to come in and shut the door. We told him that we both had doctor's appointments the next morning: Tim to see if he was going to have to go on kidney dialysis, and me to have an ultrasound on my left leg to see if I had a blood clot.

George said the most comforting and beautiful prayer. Before he left, he hugged me and shook Tim's hand. We both felt so much better about the situations and we just knew everything was going to be alright.

The next morning I got up at 9:30. After my normal morning routine I went to lunch in the dining room and then back to my hallway. Tim came from his room with an umbrella. It was raining and he had to wait for the bus while I waited on the ambulance. The ambulance took me before Tim left on his bus.

They took me to Jackson General Madison County Hospital. I was there for quite awhile. I got back just before supper. I saw Tim not long after I got back, though he said he had been back for a little while. I asked about his tests, and he asked me about mine. We just knew everything would be alright. We were tired and so thankful.

Another morning I was awakened at 7:10 a.m. for blood work, which I really do not care for. When I had been in the trauma unit at the Med, every time I turned around they were drawing blood, so I got to where I dreaded just the thought of it.

After a normal day of meals and activity, I stayed in the hall and walked from 7 to 8 p.m. I walked as much as I could. I never found out the results of that blood work. I guess they were checking my sugar since it had been awhile since it had been checked.

A few nights later I woke up at 1:00 in the morning and threw up all over myself. I am not sure what was wrong; maybe I had a touch of a stomach virus. My head was hurting and I was so sick to my stomach. Everyone came in and checked on me to see what I needed. They checked my sugar level which was fine. I tried to go back to sleep but my headache kept me awake.

When I knew I was going to throw up again I tried to sit on the side of the bed but I missed the garbage can and threw up on the floor. Instead of changing my sheets, the staff had to clean the floor instead. I finally went to sleep.

I needed to get up early as Jim and Gary were coming for our visit; I always looked forward to my boys' visits.

After they arrived, I was still not feeling well and still had a headache. We went to the dining room for lunch and back to my room. We said our goodbyes and I went back to bed for the rest of the day.

Good News!

I felt much better the next day, so I walked the hallway five times at different times of the day. Dorothy came to my room and we talked about setting a goal for me to be able to go home.

I was so excited that I would be leaving soon, but at the same time I was upset and not looking forward to the day I would have to tell my lifetime friend, Tim, goodbye.

With the goal of going home in mind, though I was not feeling good a few days later, I got up at 6:30 a.m. determined to enjoy my day. I went to the dining room for breakfast for the first time, and then went back for lunch. After this I had a shower, shampooed my hair and dried it. At 1:30 there was a cakewalk in the dining room, so Tim and I went and sat together. The employees had paid for their tickets so they could win a cake. Some of the cakes were store bought and some were homemade.

I was in my wheelchair until they started playing music. I then got up, and as they walked around the cakewalk to the music, I clapped my hands and danced a little, watching each employee and hoping their number would be the one the music stopped on.

The first couple of times when the music stopped no one was on a number, so they started the music again. It took awhile before anyone ended on a number. Once they did, the staff let different patients draw numbers to see who had won. If a patient wanted to walk they could, so a few did, or used their wheelchairs. I remember laughing at Betty and Dorothy. They wanted to win so badly! I think Dorothy won, but Betty did not. Every now and then someone would win two or even three cakes. We all got a cupcake while we were watching; it was good. I enjoyed the day after all.

Surprise!

The next time Jim and Gary came to visit, Jim told the kitchen staff there would be four for lunch. To my surprise our daughter, Penny, and son-in-law, Robin, had spent the night in Jackson. Penny had brought me a nice card about mothers. It was a good day and a nice surprise. Of course they did not know that after they all left I read the card and cried.

On Valentine 's Day, I got up at 5:30 am, ate breakfast in my wheelchair then took a shower and shampooed and dried my hair. Jim and Penny spent the morning with me. Jim had brought me a card and flowers. They stayed a little while then headed back home.

I went to the dining room for lunch then Lisa came to walk with me. When we came back to my room, I told her I needed to go to the bathroom. I thought she had locked my chair but when I went to get into it, it went out from under me.

Karen, the wound care nurse, was coming down the hall and saw what had happened, so she went and got help. They had to use the lift to get me off of the floor. Once they got me back in my chair I asked them to let me see if I could walk. I did not know if I was hurt or not. Thankfully, I was not.

It was almost time for our Valentine's Day party to begin. Since I was not badly hurt, I went to the party—and I was so glad! They had voted in a king and queen of the healthcare facility, and guess what? Neil was crowned king and I was crowned queen! We each got a box of sugar-free candy and had Valentine cookies and punch. We also got a glass with a heart on it. Shirley took pictures of us. It was one of the best days of my life. As an obese person, I had never imagined anything like this ever happening to me— but it did!

Here are pictures of myself and Neil (who has since passed away) after being voted and crowned "King and Queen for the Day." My current weight was 401 lbs.

Time Is Running Out

I was really beginning to look forward to going home. One day not long after Valentine's, everyone wanted to go to lunch at Burger King. I asked Shirley if she would bring me a chicken sandwich if I gave her some money. I gave her enough money for my chicken sandwich plus enough extra to take two other patients that did not have the money to go.

I took my shower and shampooed my hair while they were gone, and then I ate my sandwich when they got back. After lunch, Tim got permission to take me outside. We stayed for 30 minutes then we went to my room, watched a little television and ate supper.

I walked a lot that night, sometimes by myself and sometimes Tim walked with me. He talked about his wife, Molly, and how much he loved and missed her. I talked about my husband and how much we missed each other, and how I was looking forward to seeing my home again, and my dear, sweet brother, my Mom Bea, my friends from the beauty shop, the customers, and all my loved ones. We also reminisced about the television shows we had enjoyed together, our walks, eating peanut butter and crackers, but most of all our friendship and how much we would miss seeing each other every day. We both thanked God for putting us together here.

Win Some, Lose Some

One morning when I got back to my room after showering, a patient from down the hall named Ray (who looked a lot like my dad) was in my bed. I finally got him up and sent him down the hall to his own room. It was sad how he would always go into the wrong rooms. If I saw that he did not know where he was going, I would tell someone and they would take him back to his room.

The man in the room across from mine could not read. When I went to play Bingo at 2:00 that day, I convinced him to come play with me. I explained that we would go together, and I would help him play his cards. Shirley let us play until everyone won a game and we each got a snack. That day we got a Little Debbie's Nutty Buddy Bar. We played Coverall together, and we won! We were the first to get Bingo and we got $1.25. I took the money and gave it to Louis to buy us Diet Cokes out of the machine. It was a fun day.

A few days later, instead of waiting for someone to wheel me to the dining room for lunch, I decided to try to do it on my own, which was a bad decision. There was a steep ramp I had to go down to get to the dining room. I should have waited for help, but I thought I could do it. I hurt my toe; somehow it got run over by one of my wheels. I guess you cannot win them all.

CHAPTER SIX

Finally Home Again!

Last Day at the Healthcare Facility

Tuesday, February 22, 2005, was my last day at the healthcare facility. I was up at 5:30 a.m. waiting in the doorway in my wheelchair for breakfast at 7:45. After lunch and a few naps I went back to the dining room for a pancake social the staff was cooking. I sat at a table with Tim, Will and Laura. I ate three pancakes with no sugar, syrup and one sausage patty. Tim said he ate about six pancakes and a sausage patty. Will said he ate about a dozen pancakes and three sausage patties. He wanted more but they finally had to tell him no. Laura said she ate about seven or eight pancakes and I cannot remember how many sausage patties. It was a feast!

Tim and I went back to my room to watch our favorite soap opera from 6:00-7:00. I knew I would miss it; the show was just not the same if we did not watch it together. Afterwards, we watched the movie "An Officer and a Gentleman." We then said our final goodnight.

I talked on the phone to my husband, then I tried to go to sleep—but I was so excited about going home the next day that I got back into my wheelchair and sat from 11:30 p.m.

until 1:00 a.m. Finally I turned on my gospel music and fell asleep.

Saying Goodbye

I was finally going home after eight longs months of being away! It was Wednesday, February 23. I woke up to a knock on my door at 7:00 a.m. It was my CNA, Katherine, and her husband, Ed. She had left work in the morning, gone home to pick up Ed, and then came back to spend about an hour and a half with me before I went home.

I ate breakfast, got showered and dressed, and then my sweet Tim got up early so he could spend the morning with me.

My husband called at about 10:30 to let me know he was on his way to get me. I called him back to ask if we could stay long enough to eat our last lunch with my buddy Tim and of course he said yes.

I was excited about going home. I was finally going to be back with my family, but at the same time it was hard to leave for I had made another family at Healthcare. Of course I had to cry because I did not know how long it would be before I would be able to see all of my new family again.

On Our Way

The ride home was good. It was the first ride in a long time without being in an ambulance and without lots of pain. It felt so good to be in our van and on the way to my house.

At home, it was so good to see my ramp on my front porch. The first thing I had to do was check out my new bathroom. It had been fixed with a new shower instead of the old bathtub, just for me. The phone rang and it was my dear, sweet Mom Bea...then I knew for sure I was home.

Later on, my brother, Dell, came to see me. It broke my heart, since I had not seen him in awhile. He had lost most of his hair and he had a black rag on his head. I could tell he had been very sick from his chemo treatments and it took everything I had in me to keep from crying. He came back later that night with dinner for all of us to eat while we spent time together.

Jim, Dell, Gary and I really enjoyed the night. We laughed, talked and looked forward to many more dinners after this one.

Returning to Routine

The first week I was home Dell would pick up food for Jim, Gary, himself and me. Sometimes Pat Underwood would come eat with us. I would call Dell and he would bring enough food for all. After we ate, I talked on the phone to Mom Bea to tell her goodnight.

Pat Underwood would visit and we would talk about Terry, who had died while I was still in Jackson. It had been hard for Pat and me. Since I was not able to go to his funeral, it just did not seem real that he was not around. We would cry, laugh and pray together, for we both missed his sweet smile and sense of humor.

I continued to have therapy; they came to the house twice a week. One therapist took my vital signs: my blood pressure and temperature—and she had me do a few leg exercises and walk a little for her. The male therapist had me do exercises, sometimes with a rubber band that he hooked up at my front door, sometimes with clothespins for my left hand and arm, sometimes playing with pink therapy putty for my hand.

I got a new doctor who was set up through Tenn-Care Health Insurance. She got me started on a few different medicines, but for the most part the same drugs I had been on.

Setback

I began having a rough time. I was constantly complaining because I was in pain all the time. When I went back to the doctor I told her what was going on. They set up another appointment for me at a pain clinic.

The pain clinic doctor was one of the most unfriendly doctors I have ever been to in my life. He told me that if I did not have gastric bypass surgery to lose weight I would never live to see 60 years old because of my morbid obesity. I wanted to lose the weight so bad, and I wanted relief from my constant pain. I took this medicine he put me on. He did not tell me, however, that I could never come off of this medicine. He had me taking two or three Methadone a day. I knew nothing about this drug other than what he had told me—that it would make me drowsy for about the first two months until my system got used to it.

I was taking two pills a day and sleeping a lot, so I decided to quit taking the Methadone cold turkey. The next thing I knew my husband had to call the police—not once but twice—and they finally took me by ambulance again to the Med. I only remember bits and pieces of how I was acting, which I will not go into. I would rather put all that behind me, for I have a wonderful life again.

Salvation in the Midst of Tragedy

One of the hardest phone calls I have ever gotten in my life was from my brother. He called me at 9:15 one morning to tell me he was at West Clinic waiting for Peggy to bring him a wheelchair because he could not walk, his leg was so swollen. He had had a hard time just putting on his jeans. Before he hung up, I told him to be sure to have Peggy call me as soon as she knew what was going on.

It was the longest 20 minutes I have ever endured until she called. She let me know they were running a CAT scan. He had a blood clot in his leg; she said she would call me later and let me know what else was going on.

The first thing they did was admit him to the hospital; he needed to stay off his leg for at least five days. We all knew how hard this would be. He was not used to being laid up.

As if that was not bad enough, the phone rang again later in the day. Peggy was crying so hard it was difficult to understand her. They had just found out he had a blood clot in his lung as well. She gave Dell the phone. He was crying so hard all he could say was, "Promise me, Genie, that you will take care of Peggy." I promised and he hung up.

When I hung up I was crying so hard myself that at first I could not tell my husband why I was so upset. We talked for a few minutes, then I decided to call my neighbor, Cindy. She did not answer her phone; she and James had changed phones and he was on the road driving. He knew something was wrong so he got in touch with Cindy and within minutes she was at my house to see what was going on.

I asked Cindy to call my niece, Dell's only daughter, Michelle, to let her know what was going on. After Cindy left I went to my room and I lost it. Jim came to check on me and then we both lost it. We were both crying so hard; the thought of losing my sweet, dear brother was more than we could bear. In the midst of this, Michelle called; Cindy had left her a message. I was so upset; I was plum mean to her. I hung up on her not once, but twice!

Later on, Jim and I were eating supper at the dining room table and the doorbell rang. It was our grandson,

Steven. I asked Jim to please take him to the barn out back. I had not seen him since I had come home and I knew Steven would know there was something wrong. My face and nose were so red from crying.

I was still sitting at the table trying to eat when there was another knock on the door. It was my friend, Pat Underwood. I told her what was going on with Dell. Then the phone rang and it was Steven's grandmother, Beth. She had not known Steven was at my house.

Steven and Jim came back in while Beth was talking to Pat, then Steven went home. It was good to see him; he had grown up and matured since the last time I had seen him. Jim sat down in his recliner, I was in my wheelchair and Pat sat in the chair next to me. I decided to call and talk to Benny and Mary Welch. Mary had recovered from her brain injury and was now in a wheelchair. Benny put me on speakerphone so Mary could hear too. She knew how upset I was so she got on the phone and asked me to accept the Lord into my life. I did and Jesus saved me in my living room as I sat in my wheelchair. I thank God for His salvation plan and for being born again!

CHAPTER SEVEN

Personal Reflections

Young Lady

There was a 12-year-old girl I knew who was abducted by a man. He put her in his car and thank God this girl was a responsible young lady. What she did saved her life. She started giving this guy "the devil," and he finally let her out of the car. Because of her wisdom, she was smart enough to not let fear overcome her in a difficult situation. Not too many of us adults would have been as smart.

She knew if he didn't let her go right then and there that she might never see her loved ones again. You were a lucky young lady and God was watching over you. Thank you, God, for taking care of this bright, young lady.

Obesity

Life with obesity was the best. God knew and now I know for it brought me where I am today.

A loving wife, mother, sister, friend, neighbor, grandma and even a great-grandma—I thank Him for this precious gift of life. It is a wonderful life through Him.

Water for Life

As Americans we are so blessed. There are places where children ask, "Is it true that in America you flush toilets with drinking water?"

I knew a boy who could not conceive how anyone could have so much clean water that they would use it to discard their waste. Water for life as Psalm 42:1 says,

As the deer pants for streams of water, so my soul pants for you, O God.

Water for life can help you get out of that pit and have that clean water we take for granted.

Pray for Our Nation

God takes good care of us. None of us walks in our President's shoes. I thank God for him. We need to pray for him, trust him, love him and thank him for taking care of our nation.

All of America needs to get back to God. We need to pray for our nation and love one another, stand and walk together as a nation. Remember to love your neighbor and love yourself.

My Heart

I give you my heart; when you hurt my heart hurts. My heart feels your pain.

When you're upset and scared I feel your pain. When I lost my dearest mother, I knew what pain, sorrow and a broken heart was. I felt like a part of me died.

I had lost a dear friend, whom I could tell all to. Mother understood me better than I understood myself. If you need a heart of love and understanding You can have my heart; I love you with all my heart.

Helping Hands

One day we met our family for lunch at Backyard Burger. We parked in a handicapped space which was on a steep incline. I thought I could make it on my own. My husband took my wheelchair in, then when I tried to make it up this hill; I knew I was going to need a helping hand. About this time, a man came along. I asked him for help; he gave me his hand and his wife took my other hand. Thank God for helping hands. If you need a helping hand, ask and ye shall receive.

The Pepsi Man

One hot day while I was waiting in a parking lot. A Pepsi truck pulled up next to my van. The young driver told me he stopped to cool off before he made his next Pepsi delivery. He was eating a bag of M&M peanuts. We talked about how hot it had been and he said he was trying to make his last delivery before it got any hotter. He was a nice man who talked about his kids. He said he expected the same from himself as he did from his kids. He talked about how many Pepsis he had to deliver and how difficult it was to get the hired help to work. He had 40 cases to deliver and I thought that was a lot for one employee to deliver. He said that was nothing compared to the order he usually had which was anywhere from 100 to 150 cases. Then my husband came out and the Pepsi man said goodbye. He made me feel good and I made him fill good. Be sure to take the time out of your busy day to make someone else feel good today. They will remember you.

Losing Weight With the Lord's Help

Give your weight over to the Lord. No matter how many times the doctors tell you the only way you will ever lose is to have gastric by-pass surgery, don't do it. Be careful because this may lead you to another habit such as drinking, drugs, or being too sexually active. In my lifetime, I've tried so many different diets that that word is like a cuss word. Instead of saying you are dieting, learn to give your weight problem to the Lord. He will put you on a new journey and free you from the bondage of the old one.

On the Lord's journey with Him in control, and letting him take care of your life's problems, you will no longer look to food. Letting Him carry that extra burden that seems overwhelming. I carried that burden for almost 50 years and now I never walk alone in this journey I am on.

And God will never let you be pushed past your limit. 1 Corinthians 10:13 indicates that He'll always be there to help us through it. Mark 10:27 promises us, "God can do all things...."

Making Lifetime Memories

From the beginning of life we start with nothing and when we leave this life we take a lifetime of memories to our heavenly home. Life is a precious treasure. It lasts for only a moment. We should enjoy one breath at a time. Look back over the years of life and think of all the different people who have come and gone. Some were lonely and sad but for the moment. We have times where love, joy, peace and good health abound. In our lifetime we have that blessed assurance we will again have precious memories that will last forever in our heavenly home with the love of God and our loving families forever.

If Only

For two small words they sure do say a lot.

As a child we say, "If only I were a teenager."

As a teen we say, "If only I was an adult."

As a young adult we say, "If only I was married."

As a spouse we say, "If only I had children."

We live our lives saying these two words over and over again because we are never satisfied. Nothing on earth can satisfy our deepest longing...only God can. Take a moment and thank Him because with Him we never have to say "If only." Learn to trust His love and His plans for your life. They are so much better than your ideas. Be content. Long to see God. Look for Him for He's looking for you.

Time

Time with the Lord brings joy to my heart. The time I spend with Him is precious. The time I spend with my soul mate, brothers, sisters, children, grandchildren, neighbors and friends is precious to me. We are here only for a moment, so let's take time to enjoy His love, grace, mercy and all the beauty wrapped up in this lifetime.

Take time for those who are in pain; take time for your neighbors, take time to visit or call those in nursing homes, take time for meals with your spouse, your kids and other family members and friends. Remember the Lord took time for each of us.

He loves and cares for all of us.

Casting all your care upon Him—for He cares
for you.

1 Peter 5:7

My Delight in God

My delight in God every day is starting my day with Him in prayer each morning with my first cup of coffee and observing the beauty He has created for us to enjoy.

I look forward to whatever the day brings, whether it be slow or busy, I know God is my strength for the day. He is with me mind, body and soul leading me in His ways with all His loving care and where He leads me I will follow forever.

Heaven to Me

Heaven to me is every breath I take and every step I take. It is my loving husband, Jim, my brothers, sister, family, neighbors, morning prayer, church time, quiet breakfast, taking a walk, exercising, enjoying each day as it happens. It is looking forward to a special time each day, seeing different people I come in contact with, talking on the phone, reading, yes, even going to the doctor. A child's smile brings such joy to me, going to the beauty shop, going to the nursing home where my Ma-Ma Bea lives and going to the healthcare facility. It is even staying there six months. Heaven to me is fixing dinner for family and friends, eating out with family and friends, writing poems, short stories and writing my first book, *It's a Wonderful Life, Again!* Heaven is cooking my special dessert, loving each person on this earth and knowing someday I'll be in heaven with my Heavenly Father, forever in eternity.

I'll Never Walk Alone

During the most difficult time of my life God took that adversity to refine me, mold me, shape me and prepare me for the plans He had to come into my life.

God knew His child needed to be off her feet to get her back where He wanted His child. Believe me when I say I would go through all the pain again to be where I am today. I praise God for my open book wound; I now call it my open Bible wound and I'll never walk alone for I have my Heavenly Father forever.

Queen for a Day

The healthcare facility voted for King and Queen. Neil was voted King and I was voted Queen. We both received crowns, sugar-free candy, balloons, a special glass to drink our punch in and I received beautiful flowers. This event occurred on Valentine's Day. My husband and daughter came and honored me with a special Valentine card. This was the most memorable Valentine's Day I had ever experienced and it made me feel beautiful in so many ways.

Jesus Opened Up My Life

Jesus came into my life of pain to save me from my sin yet He never sinned. But He took the pain of the cross. Jesus opened my life and set me free from my sin on what I thought was the day from hell. I cried out for His help and He came into my living room where I sat in my wheelchair talking and crying to a friend on the phone about the day I had had and all the pain and disappointments in my life. She asked me to ask the Lord to come into my life and I did. It was "the" experience of my lifetime. I felt like the weight of the world had been taken off my shoulders.

I felt so much love for my Lord and Savior. I thank Him every day for opening up my life to Him. I'm free at last and forever. Let Jesus open up your life forever.

One Day at a Time

Dell is free of colon cancer. Our granddaughter had ovarian cancer at 13 and again at 15 years of age and now at 17, see is cancer free! Our friend Mary got off of life support and is alive and well today. I was given odds of not being able to walk again or being able to lose weight if I didn't have gastric bypass surgery. Today, I have beat those odds and am walking and have lost weight with God's help. Miracles happen everyday just in the way we breathe, walk, talk, see, and hear. Even getting out of bed every day is a miracle in itself. Enjoy your miracles and the life God has in store for you...one day at a time.

Piles of Ashes

Put your pile of ashes in God's hands. Every morning give Him your awakening thoughts. My pile of ashes is my weight problem that I need to give to God every hour I am awake. Only God can change my pile of ashes. He waits expecting, looking and longing to be gracious to me. I lift Him up so that He will have mercy on me. He shows lovingkindness to me. God turns my pile of ashes into beauty...beauty for ashes.

Willing Heart

God's love is in me, I am not perfect, I just have a willing heart. God's love is in me. He steps in and helps me just because I am His child. God sees me as a brand new creation because the old has passed away. Start looking at what lies ahead in your life with a willing heart. God makes miracles out of our messes.

Love Child

God is awesome!

I know of friends who have been waiting on a child for a long time. One day God brought them a love child. We all gave God praise and glory for the blessing of this little one for we knew it was going to be spoiled. Besides, that is what should happen. We praised God from whom all blessings flow. As God's children, we are richly and unceasingly blessed by Him. God is good. Amen.

My Riches

My riches are in knowing Christ. I have riches in His salvation, riches in His forgiveness, riches in His joy, riches in His peace, riches in His glory, riches in His honor, riches in His majesty, riches in His love for me, and I am blessed. I have true prosperity in my everyday life and I declare I am truly rich.

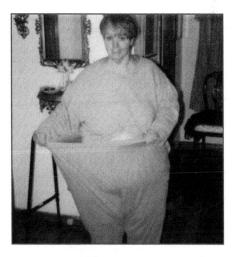

Here I am at 373 lbs., having lost 121 lbs.

CHAPTER EIGHT

Friends for Life

Tim

Tim is my wonderful lifelong friend. God had a plan and put us together in the same place at the same time for a reason. God knew our situations. He knew Tim had lost his dear wife, Molly on June 8, 2004. God also knew I was in a place where I had no one I loved—no family, no friends—until Tim and I met.

Tim and I were both emotional people who cared deeply for life. We touched each other's lives within our souls and we will always be wonderful friends. Isaiah 9:6 tells us, "His name will be called Wonderful, Counselor, Mighty God, Everlasting Father, Prince of Peace."

One of the reasons Tim and I met each other was because of the love we received from our certified nursing assistant (CNA), Katherine. She introduced the two of us. After we met, we looked forward to seeing each other every day. We talked about everything; Tim is a good listener and I knew he was interested in what I was saying. I talked about how many years I had prayed for God to send me someone regardless of my obesity. I told him how my husband, Jim, and I had met; about our children and grandchildren; my brother Dell; the death of my mother, Rose; my daddy, Raymond; my godmother, Mom Bea; our Aunt Kaky (Kathleen); my friends; the beauty shop; and about having to quit doing hair and going on disability after 30 years.

Tim knows me pretty well. We are kind of alike, except he is much quieter. We are both emotional people. We would watch "Extreme Makeover" on TV and if he cried, I cried or if I cried, he cried. We would say we were not going to watch it again but of course we would. The thing about watching TV with Tim was if I was talking to him, he would listen to me instead of watching TV.

We both have a thing for peanut butter. I thought I liked it, but believe me he even had me beat on that. We went to lots of different activities together. We played Bingo, ate popcorn at the socials. We went to the pancake social. We did most of our socializing in my room together—sometimes alone and sometimes with all of our friends.

One night Tim was in my room watching TV. I had gone for a walk. He came out looking for me and he said, "You scared me. I did not see you when I looked out in the hall."

There were lots of evenings when we sat in the hallway by the front door while everybody else had gone to bed. Everybody there went to bed with the chickens and got up with the chickens. Tim and I were not early risers. We liked to stay up late, then sleep later in the mornings, especially on the mornings we had pain.

There were a few times when Tim scared me. He had a spell with his arm and hand which he could not control, that was much of the reason he was not big on visiting with others. With me he was relaxed and did not let his problem keep him from seeing me. He knew I cared for him and understood that we all have problems with our health, some more than others. It was nice to know someone cared. I have always been one who feels someone else's pain; I do not like to see someone else hurting. Whenever they hurt I hurt.

Tim and I never dwelt on our pain; we just kept on getting up and helped each other.

I love you, my wonderful lifelong friend, Tim.

My First Friend, Pete Hansen

I met Pete as he was coming down the hall. He looked in and went on down the hall. When he came back by my room, I asked him to come in, so he did. It was hard to understand at first what he was saying or talking about, but as time passed I could understand most of what he was telling me.

He told me his name was Pete Hansen—not handsome, but handsome to me. He thought that was funny. He said he was from Alabama, and that years ago, when he was in the eleventh grade, he had been in a car wreck. He had not seen his three brothers and one sister; he told me their names.

Just about everyday he would come to see me; sometimes he talked, but most of the time I did the talking. I told him about my life and family. He met my husband, my cousin and my brother. I introduced him to one of my first girl-friends, little Laura.

Laura

Laura arrived at the healthcare facility not long after I did. She was in the room down the hall on the opposite side. We became good friends; she would come to my room and visit me at least once, sometimes two or three times a day.

Laura was the type of person who liked to help others, which got her into trouble quite often. She got things off my shelf that I could not get for myself. She would get in trouble for not wanting to use her walker. She would bring my toothpaste and toothbrush and then she would go wash them out for me. We helped each other as much as we could.

Laura helped me during a very hard time of my life. It was difficult for me to need to have this much help. She would hang up clothes, and hand me whatever I would ask for. Sometimes she would stop in to see if I needed anything and then check on me again later.

We told each other about our lives and our families. Her mother was also dead. We talked about how much we missed our mothers. We talked about different situations in our lives. We laughed a lot, cried together, and there were times we prayed together.

One day Laura introduced me to a school friend, Joy. She had known her for a long time. Joy thanked me for being kind to our friend, Laura. I told her that I did not need any thanks for being Laura's friend.

We even played games on my TV trays one night, but not too late. She was an early-to-bed girl. Not long after we met, I introduced her to Pete. He came by to visit and Laura was there; I thought they both needed someone in their lives.

Bill

On my first day while my husband Jim was unpacking my things, some of the other patients told me about a man named Bill. They said he was bad about picking up things that did not belong to him. He was not supposed to come into any other person's room without their permission. Jim put some of my things that were on the shelves into my drawers instead, to keep them safe.

Later, when I met Bill, he came in on his own. He picked up this and that. I told him that these things were mine and he should put them down, so he did. As we became friends he would come to my door and sometimes I would ask him in. Other times I told him I was not feeling well and he respected me, as I did him.

Bill was a lonely but kind person. He always talked to anyone who came in the front door. He did most of those things for attention.

Sheila

Sheila walked the hallway every day. She stopped by, or sometimes came in for a second and then out the door she would go. Other times she would come in, sit down for and a bit, and then leave. There were times she would talk, but she was usually quiet. However, if she got hungry you could hear her at the opposite end of the hall. She would yell, "I'm hungry!" and you certainly understood what she was saying. The CNA would tell her to get up and go to the kitchen for a cheese sandwich, but she would not go unless the CNA took her.

If I knew Sheila was hungry, I would tell her to come to my room. She would eat peanut butter and crackers, animal crackers, Fig Newton's, candy or whatever I had on the shelves. She just liked junk food.

One weekend I was watching a Richard Gere movie and she came in and saw him kissing a lady on the screen. All of sudden she said with a smile, "I love kissing."

I said, "Sheila, I think you are like me; you think he is really good looking." Every time after this, if I mentioned Richard, she would grin and we would both laugh. I told some of the CNAs about this and they did not believe me. So I told them "Watch this." I asked Sheila, "Do you think Richard Gere is sexy and good looking?" She lit up with a big, old smile and we all laughed.

Joyce

Joyce was very quiet most of the time. She did not talk a lot, but when we were alone she would talk about her daughter and how much she loved and missed her.

Joyce loved to visit me and I enjoyed our visits. There were times she would come to my room before I was even up. We would eat peanut butter and crackers with Laura, Bill, Sheila and Louis. She would eat, then go on her way.

She got sent to another health care; I missed her and still think of her.

Rod

Rod was also from Memphis. He was in an accident a few days after my accident. He was run over while crossing a street. He had to have surgery on his head and have his arm sewn back on at the elbow. He was at the Med Hospital in Memphis when I was, but we never ran across each other that we know of.

At the healthcare facility, Rod's room was at the end of my hallway. We met not long after I got there. He came to see me every day at least once and sometimes more. He would let me know what we were having for lunch or supper. He often used my cell phone to call his girlfriend. He missed her and I understood that.

Rod had therapy like I did. He used the clothespins, and at one time he had some special kind of instrument he had to use on his fingers. It helped move them better. We often talked about our therapy; we had the same therapist. She would ask me about Rod and him about me.

The therapist told me Rod did not mind the clothespins. I do not know exactly how much pain he had, but for me, using the clothespins was the hardest exercise. Rod did not like the way I put them back on the board. I could tell when he had used them, and he could tell when I had used them. I thought Rod would go home before Christmas, but it turned out I got to go home before he did.

Thelma

Thelma was in the last room on the opposite side of the hall. She was married to Don; they had 13 children. When she first arrived she could not walk because she had a broken hip, so she had surgery. I could tell she was doing her therapy; at first she moved slowly but each day as she passed my room I could see she was improving a little each time.

Thelma's daughter, Tiffany, would walk her. Sometimes her sons walked her. I would see different family members walking her at different times. Thelma was always having company. I met her sister, her daughters and a few of her grandchildren.

Tiffany came almost every night, and she and I became friends. She would always look in on me just like she did her mother. She always stopped and talked and told me goodnight before she left. As time went by, Thelma's husband, Don, would stop by for a few minutes to visit with me or he would wave at me and tell me goodnight as he passed my room.

One night Thelma wanted some mayonnaise on something we had for supper, so Tiffany came to my room to see if I had any mayonnaise. I told her where it was on the shelf in a container. She found it, but there was only one package left. She said, "I'm not going to take it because it's your last"; but I insisted.

The next day Tiffany came and took Thelma shopping. When they got back, Tiffany stopped in and handed me a sack, and in that sack was a jar of salad dressing, which I prefer over mayonnaise. She would not let me pay her. This is the kind of family they were; they were all very thoughtful of others and they loved one another deeply.

One time I met another of Thelma's relatives, a lady and her children. We talked and she introduced her kids. There were several unusual names in the family. Some of them I could not pronounce, much less try to spell.

As Thelma's therapy improved, she would get in her wheelchair, wheel past my room and sit in the hall so she could look out the front door. On the way back to her room she would stop and talk a little. She was a good listener, probably because she had so many kids.

There were a few times when I saw Thelma on her walker; it would make me long to get back up on my feet again. Thelma finally got to go home; I was proud of her and happy for Don and her loving children, but it took me a while to get used to not seeing Thelma and her dear family every day. This family touched my life in such a special way and I thank God for each of them.

Todd (Pa-Paw)

Todd was a little black man who had one leg. He stayed in his wheelchair out in the hall at the front door looking out. Everyone called him Little Todd, but I called him Pa-Paw.

When I was in the hall we would talk, and when I was finally able to go to the dining room, I was assigned a seat at Pa-Paw's table. One day I sat with three other ladies at the first table as you come in, and Pa-Paw said, "What are you doing over there?" I told him Laura was eating in her room and I was going to eat with the ladies, but I would be back at our table again the next day.

One day when we were in the hall Pa-Paw asked me if he could have a hug. Of course I wanted a hug too and from then on we often gave each other hugs.

Charles, Doug, Ken and Ace

Charles and Doug were roommates for awhile, then Charles moved in with Ken. They were on my hall. I would often see Charles and Ken going down the hall to go outside and smoke. Ken would stop in occasionally to talk for a little bit, then later on they got him a remote wheelchair so he could get around easier. Doug always wanted to take a walk so the CNAs would help him try to walk even though he had a hard time.

One day Doug and I played cards out in the hall close to the front door so we could see out. He won both games; he thought that was so funny.

Charles was paralyzed from the neck down. He had been in a car accident. He really was a sweetheart, even though he did not want anyone to know. He loved his mother, daddy and sister. They would come and visit him; sometimes they would get him out for a couple of hours.

Ace was also paralyzed from the waist down, due to a robbery where he got shot somehow. Ace and Charles would come visit me late at night when everyone else was sleeping. We would watch a movie on my VCR. We enjoyed watching our movies; sometimes we would eat popcorn that someone popped in the microwave for us.

Ace and Charles were both good-looking young men. Rod, Charles, Ken and A. J. would often pass my room on the way to go out to smoke. Each one of them would check on me quite often, so I never had much time on my hands to get too lonely.

Lina

Lina was an older black woman in the room next to mine. She came by my room every day. She was always going out to smoke. Sometimes she would stop in and we would talk

77

about her son and my family. Her son would come in from Mississippi once a month and take her shopping or to get her hair fixed; she loved when he would take her to get ice cream.

I would often buy Lina a Coke or give her one off my shelf if I had any. She loved candy, so I would give her sugar-free candy occasionally. She brought me peppermints once, and she gave me a bar of soap for a Christmas present.

Louis

Louis was in the room across the hall from me. He visited some every day unless he was going to church on Sunday with his sister. She would come and take him out for the weekend; if she had time, she checked in on me.

Louis liked to come to my room. We ate peanut butter and crackers or I would give him food that my Aunt Kaky had sent. She always sent extra for me to share. He ate animal crackers, cookies, candy, popcorn and chips, and he would go to the kitchen for ice cream until they put a stop to this. He was a diabetic so I tried to watch how much I let him eat. His sister would leave him money to get a Coke and I would let him have one.

Sometimes we would sit in the hall, if he could find a chair to bring into the hall. He had a bit of a temper. Sometimes we would get upset with each other. He would go on his way, and then we would both cool down and talk again as if nothing had happened.

I was often afraid I had hurt his feelings—that was never my intention. We were both hard-headed, but also friends.

Glen

Glen shared a room with Louis. He seldom got to come out of his room. They put him in a special chair so he could go to the dining room, but most of the time he made too much noise. At times he got to visit in the hall in that same special chair.

I would go in his room and we would talk a few minutes; sometimes we talked from our beds across the hall from each other—we could see each other. Bill would also go into Glen's room and talk. I thought that was kind, though I am not sure if they understood each other.

Glen's brother, Frank, would come to see him. He would bring his guitar and play in Glen's room and they would sing together. I could tell Glen enjoyed this. Sometimes Frank would play his guitar for me and whoever happened to be out in the hall with me.

When Frank would come and see me in my room, and ask me how I was doing, I would ask him, "How is Glen doing?" One time Frank came to my room and I said a prayer for Glen. I kept both of them in my prayers, especially for Frank when he went home. They were from somewhere in Alabama.

Will

Will was in the same hallway not too far down on the opposite side. He shared a room with Bill and someone else. Will was quiet so when we first met, we only talked if we happened to be in the hall. One day I told him to go into my room. He wanted a Coke, so he got one. Another day Joyce, Louis and Will ate Fig Newton's that Aunt Kaky had sent with Jim.

As time went by, and I was doing better, I would sit in my wheelchair and eat supper in my doorway, waiting on Tim to come back from supper and a smoke. One night Will came up behind me, put his around my neck and gave me a big hug, which I enjoyed. We all need hugs.

Sara and James

Sara was in the last room on my side of the hall. She stayed in her wheelchair most of the time, though she was able to walk a little. When she passed by me in the hall, I would see her get out of her chair and walk to the bathroom. She had had several strokes and her fingers were locked up on her.

Sara loved to primp. She was always fixing her hair, putting on makeup and dressing up, especially on Sundays or when a friend or her brother came to see her or to take her out for a while. She used to tell me all the time that she wished she had my natural beauty, which I loved to hear. She would tell me I was a queen; she was always complimenting me about something.

She had a special friend, also a friend of mine, another James who went by the name "James" rather than "Jim." I would often see them pass by my room on the way to her room. One day he helped her rearrange her room. He put her bed and her things the way she wanted them. She asked me to come down and see her room; she was thrilled about how pretty it looked.

Sometimes she would come by my room at night and visit with Tim and me for a few minutes, and then she and James would go out to smoke again before going to bed. She would usually tell me goodnight unless she happened to fall asleep.

One day we went to exercises. Shirley put on some music and I was feeling good, so I got her and James to dance together. In the meantime, I was dancing with another friend, Darrell. I tried to get more people involved with our fun but no one else would dance. They enjoyed watching us.

I looked out into the dining room and saw Betty looking in the mirror. She is the head of the health center. I thought to myself, "Oh no," but to my surprise she opened the door and started dancing a little herself. After she left, I saw a different CNA looking in; others came in and said, "You sure are having fun, aren't you?" We were. It was a good time for all of us.

Neil

I was in the hallway in my wheelchair one day, waiting on my therapist to return to walk me. She had said, "Whatever you do; do not get up on your own"; so I was just sitting. This man came by with overalls on. I told him, "I like your overalls and I wish I had a pair."

He replied, "But you are too big to be wearing them" and he went on. The next day, I was in the hall again, only this time he told me, "Miss, I should not have said what I said to you."

I told him the only reason I had not said anything back was because he had hurt my feelings and I was afraid I would say something mean that I could not take back. After this we became friends. We would often talk, and he ate lunch at the same table with Pa-Paw, Dick and I. Neil was popular and everyone there liked him. He was voted king of the healthcare facility.

Lance

Lance was also from Memphis. He was a nice, young, black man who had been shot years before. He was paralyzed. He would wheel by my room in his chair, usually flirting with one of the ladies, and he would stop in and talk. He told me he wanted to talk to his mother so occasionally he would use my cell phone to call her.

Darrell

Darrell was always popping his fingers to the beat of the music. He had a good rhythm. At exercise class he was the first one I got to get up and dance with me. I stood in front of my wheelchair and danced, then I finally got Sara and James to join us. Of course I had to push them to join in. James was a little shy until he got started. At times we all four danced together.

Darrell would walk the halls during the day, and at nighttime he would come by my room. He would forget where his room was, so I would tell him, "Darrell, you are on the second hall" and I would give him his room number. Occasionally, we would sit in the hall at night. I would do the talking and he would do the listening. If I had extra change, I would buy him a Dr. Pepper.

My Friend, Ali

Ali was a sweet, funny, black lady. She would come into my room and say, "How are you, Nurse?" I have no idea why she thought I was a nurse because I was in bed. I told her I was a patient living there, doing my rehab.

I was told that when she first came she was mildly undernourished and needed to put on weight so they let her eat what she could. However, by the time I arrived, they told me to watch how much food I gave her. She would come in my room and would ask if she could have anything she saw on my shelves. One night there were five things she wanted. I told her to take the can of tomato juice and one other thing to eat and that was all.

One day she came in my room and I had some blankets on my shelf. She wanted to know if I cared if she folded them, so I told her she could. It took her so long! She could not get them exactly like she wanted them. She would pull them down and start over and over again. I told her to just put them up there and forget it, that it did not matter how they were folded as long as they were out of the way. She stopped folding, but before I knew it she was on the floor on the right side of my bed. She was under my dinner table! I had no idea what she was looking for. She found the side rail that went to the end of my bed, so I told her to put it down and get off the floor before she got hurt, and then she went back to her room.

Becky Hamburger

Hamburger was a lady down the hall. That was her last name, so that was what everyone called her; I even heard some people call her "Cheeseburger." She was in the same room with Ali and another lady.

Hamburger would come down the hall on the way to the restroom, and if I was in the hallway by the front door, she would stop and say something. Sometimes I understood her and other times I did not. Every now and then if I was doing my walking, she would stop and watch me.

My Friend, Sandra

Sandra was on another hall so I would see her most of the time in the dining room. She stayed mostly to herself in her bed. She had been there almost a year before I arrived and had put on almost 100 pounds. I finally got her to come to exercise class. At first she just sat and did not exercise at all. One day I told her to come and sit with Laura and me while we helped Shirley lead class. She did, and she finally did a little exercise. Shirley tried to get everyone to at least try. I told Sandra, "If I can do this, I know you can at least give it a try."

My Friends Minnie, Barbara and Patty

Minnie, Barbara and Patty ate lunch at the same table. Barbara's daughters would come and stay with her, and sometimes they would bring her a hamburger instead of what we had for lunch. She kept orange sherbet in the freezer for her lunch every day. Minnie liked to come to Bingo when she felt well enough.

Barbara's daughters were always so kind to their mother, Minnie and Patty. Minnie and Barbara were roommates while Patty was in a different room, but they brought her things too.

On weekends, Jim and Gary got to meet Barbara's girls. One of her girls was also named Barbara. She had worked there at one time and still loved to help the patients, like one little lady who was blind. She would help the lady get back down the hall and to her room.

Kevin and Ann

Kevin and Ann's room was the last room on my side of the hall. When I went on my walks and would reach the end of the hall, I would usually stop and check in on them to see how Ann felt. She was on oxygen all the time. If she came to activities, they brought her oxygen with her. She liked to play Bingo as well as we do. Kevin would come play Bingo if Ann felt O.K.

If I was in the hallway while Kevin was in his wheelchair wheeling himself to the restroom, he would always take the time to talk to me and find out how I was doing. He would tell me I was a kind young lady. After I went home, his dear wife, Ann, passed away. He ended up in the room across the hall from my friend, Tim.

Maggie

Maggie's room was the last room on the opposite side of my room. She was the oldest living person there; she was 94 years old. She sat in her wheelchair out in the hall. If she saw me in the hall, she would wave at me. When I was able to get to the end of the hall I would stop at her door and talk to her.

Maggie liked to play Bingo and sometimes she came to Bible study or whatever activity she could when she felt up to it. She was a nice lady and I liked listening to her stories. She had a string running across her room with cards she had received in the mail. We both looked forward to our cards from our friends, family and loved ones. When I went home, I left her the plant they had given me when I was crowned queen. I knew she would take better care of it than I would, and that it would live for her.

CHAPTER NINE

Staff Extraordinaire

Starting From the Top

Betty was the head of the healthcare facility; she ran the place. I am not exactly sure what all she did. She was always busy—there was always so much going on with bringing in new patients and setting up therapy. If I needed something, I would find out if she could help with what I needed; if not, I would ask one of the other employees until I found the right one to help me with what I needed.

Dorothy, Social Worker

Dorothy was the first person I met. She came to the Med to see me. I had been having problems getting a social worker to take me on. No one was willing to take me on account of my weight, until the Med contacted Dorothy. Just as I was beginning to wonder if anyone would ever accept me, Dorothy told them she would talk with me.

My friends and family and I prayed that God would send someone to help, and that was my dear friend, Dorothy. She worked with my disability lawyer to get my bills paid for and all my paperwork taken care of. She helped to get me Tenn-

Care Health Insurance; she made the appointment for my husband Jim in Jackson. She took care of my doctor appointments and transportation there and back. She took care of all my special needs.

Shirley, Activity Director

When we first met, Shirley and I liked each other. She would come and check on me even though I was not yet able to go to any activity. Every Friday before she got off for the weekend, she would come see if I needed anything. She brought me puzzle books, crossword books, Christian tapes, movies for my VCR and a big hug for the weekend.

If they had something special going on or if they had a cookout for everyone who could go out, she or someone else would bring me food. When she had happy hour outside she would make sure those of us who could not come got a non-alcoholic drink. She made strawberry daiquiris, margaritas and piña coladas; they were good.

Shirley was always thinking of all kinds of activities for us to do. We had exercise class, popcorn socials, Bingo, Bible study, singing and cookouts—sometimes hot dogs and hamburgers, one time they made barbecued bologna on the grill. Every month there were birthday parties and happy hours. We made candy, cookies, fudge, pumpkin pies, peanut butter and jelly sandwiches; one of my favorites was donut holes. They were so good!

Shirley would always try to get everyone involved. If someone did not participate, it was not for her lack of trying.

My Therapists

I had two therapists. One took care of the therapy on my legs. She was from the Philippines. The other therapist took care of my arm and left hand therapy. She had me put clothespins on a board and then take them off. This may not sound hard, but it was. I also had to take colored rings and put them together and then take them apart. This was easier than the clothespins. There were also cone-looking things that the therapist would hold. I had to take one at a time and put them on my TV tray and then put them back in her hand. Sometimes we put a red rubber band on the side arm of my bed. I would pull on it in different directions. We also played with a balloon, bouncing it back and forth to each other. I tried to use my left hand when doing this.

My leg therapy was slow at first. She had me move my feet and legs in different directions. It was slow and painful but I knew it would get better with time. Sometimes she would help me move my legs and feet; other times she put my legs on pillows and exercised them. There were days when they put me on wedges, on my left side one day and my right side the next day—it hurt! No matter what side I was on, there were times I would cry and try not to let anyone know it. Sometimes my therapists would see me crying and they would tell me "It's going to get better." Thankfully, it did.

Fran

Fran was the lady who did my laundry and brought my clothes back to my room. She was usually in and out.

Every now and then I would see her out in the hall and she would talk. She was another funny lady; she would cut up and have a good time. She was always kind and sweet to me.

Karen, Wound Care Nurse

Karen was my wound care nurse. She put Crisco on my feet every day to help with my calluses. It helped to get rid of the dead skin. Some days she would sit at the foot of my bed and scrape the dead skin off. My feet were a whole lot better. She also kept my toenails and fingernails cut.

At one point, I was put on a bedpan and developed a wound. She checked my wound and put special ointment on it which always made me feel better.

Vicki

Vicki was my morning nurse. She always helped to get my medicine and took my sugar when necessary. If I needed pain medicine, she would make sure I got it at the right time.

Vicki was not too talkative, but occasionally she did talk, mostly when I asked her questions about her family. I always talked to her about something. I love to talk.

Kathy

Kathy was the second shift nurse, a very quiet person. I never really got to know much about her. She helped as much as the other nurses. Of course, I talked to her about my family and everything else, and she was a good listener.

Linda

Linda was the nurse who worked mostly on the weekends. We talked a lot about her family; she brought pictures. We also talked about my family. She did everything for me; she cared for all my needs. Sometimes she worked during the week and helped me then too.

Wanda

Wanda was the nighttime nurse. She was the one who woke me up at about 5:30 in the morning to see what my sugar level was. There were times at night when she had to bring me my pain medicine. She changed my catheter several times for me. She could change it without any problems. I would occasionally get a bladder infection or kidney problems; she would order medication for me.

I always hated to bother Wanda, but she said it was no bother. She did not want me to be in pain, which I appreciated very much. She talked about her only son and how much she loved him.

Evonne

Evonne was a nurse on a different hall most of the time. If one of the other nurses did not come in, she would be my nurse. Sometimes she worked as my nurse on the weekends as well. She was the nicest—a very pretty lady. She always told me how pretty she thought I was. I loved her, for that made me feel pretty as well. When you are obese, most of the time you hear, "If you could only lose weight...."

CNA, Katherine, My Special CNA

Katherine was very special to me. She helped me more than words can ever say. She took care of all my needs: she shampooed my hair in bed, shaved my legs and made me as comfortable as she could. We became like mother and daughter. She loved to help me.

We talked about her family—Ed and Bob—my family, her work, my work. We could tell each other anything, our thoughts our problems. She knew about all my close friends because I was always talking about my husband, brother, Mom Bea, Aunt Kaky, all my friends at the beauty shop and my customers, Pat and Terry Underwood.

If I got bad news she and my friend, Tim, were always there to help me feel better. We cried and talked a lot; ate and played together. She could tell me if she was in pain and I would help her as she did me. Every time we saw each other we would hug each other. She knew I was here with no family and how close I was to mine, so she introduced me to my wonderful life friend, Tim. She knew he had lost his dear wife and needed a good friend, so that was me. Every night before Katherine went home she came in, told me goodnight and gave me a hug and a kiss.

Pastor George, My CNA

George was my black certified nursing assistant. He worked on the 2:00 to 10:00 p.m. shift. He was my friend and my pastor while I was at the healthcare facility.

George helped me so much while I was there. He prayed for me and my friends. He had church services on Sundays around 3:00.

I remember the first night my CNA, Katherine, came to my room. She asked me if I wanted her to show George how she always cleaned me up around 7:30 every night. She was not sure if I would have a problem with him being a black man. I had already met George and I knew this would be O.K., so I told Katherine I would appreciate her doing this.

George introduced me later on to his wife, Stephanie, who was a minister. She was also a heavyset lady and we hit it off the first time we met. She told me she would pray for me and that she knew I would get my weight off. Some weeks she came to our church services. Their family members and congregation came with them. Thank you George and Stephanie for your prayers, your concern and your love!

Terry (CNA)

Terry was my morning CNA. She took such good care of me! She used to kid me about talking. One day when she went by my room she thought I was talking to myself, but it was my little friend Laura who was sitting in a chair in the corner; Terry had not seen her when she passed my room.

Terry told me I was like the Energizer Bunny because I just kept talking and talking. We could always make each other laugh, which I needed as well as she did. Some days were stressful and we all needed laughter, a hug or just a smile. Terry quit and I missed her.

Bonnie (CNA)

Bonnie was also one of my morning CNAs. She called me "Mom" as I was old enough to be her mother. We had many fun days. We laughed; we talked about her family and friends. She made sure I got what I needed.

If either of us had a rough day, we would help each other get through the morning. She was always concerned about me, constantly smiling, very kind, gentle and loving.

Genie (CNA)

Genie worked the mornings. She was not my CNA, but she would come and check on me whenever my CNA that was on duty in the morning was busy and could not get to me. She would answer and check on me when I pushed my call bell for help.

Genie had a crazy since of humor. She could make me laugh one minute and cry the next.

Thank you, Genie, for always coming in to help me and for all the crazy things you would do in our hallway to make our days a little better!

Tony and Robert (CNAs)

Tony and Robert were both black men, which did not matter to me in any way. Tony would occasionally be my

CNA for the day. He took care of me. He always kept me in stitches; he loved to act silly—we can all use a little silliness in our lives!

Robert was a good-looking bald-headed young man with lots of muscles. He was not my CNA and did not work on my hallway, but he would help me when he came on my hall. He would come to check on me and sometimes push me to the dining room. He knew I liked to look at him, but he never let his looks go to his head. He had a beautiful wife; he showed me her picture. I asked him about his family and I told Tony and him about my family and loved ones as well.

Nita (CNA)

Nita worked in the morning from 2:00 to 10:00. She was another one with a good sense of humor. We would laugh and cut up and just have a good time.

One day she was helping me get my bath. She was holding on so I could stay on my side while someone else was washing the other side. I decided all of a sudden to reach up and tickle her. She jumped and it startled me.

From then on every time I saw her I would try to tickle her again. I had never in my life seen anyone this ticklish.

Gina (CNA)

Gina was on the 2:00 to 10:00 shift when Katherine was off of work. She usually worked the other end of the hall, but she would always come to my room and check on me.

Most of the time Katherine and Gina worked the hallway together and they took turns helping me, depending on which one answered the buzzer.

My room was the hangout room for the CNAs—different ones were always checking on me, and my room was busy with different friends visiting, coming and going.

Gina's mother made a cake once which was really good. She quit and moved to Florida with her mother.

Jerry, Lorraine and Melinda (CNAs)

Jerry, Lorraine and Melinda also worked 2:00 to 10:00. They were not my CNAs very often.

Occasionally, Jerry would take Katherine or Gina's place. She also worked at another healthcare. She was kind. She took care of my needs, as did Lorraine and Melinda.

Lorraine and Melinda worked on a different hall most of the time but they checked on me occasionally. Lorraine would sometimes be my CNA. Other times I saw them bringing supper trays down the hallway.

Tina (CNA)

Tina worked 2:00 to 10:00. When Katherine moved to the 10:00 to 6:00 slot, Tina took her place. She was a good CNA. She also worked at another healthcare. She talked about her children. They were handicapped; she loved them very much.

Tina waited on me just like Katherine, so it was not quite as bad without my Katherine being on my shift. She was quiet, sweet and helpful, concerned and saw to my needs.

Libbey (CNA)

Libbey was my nightshift CNA from 10:00 to 6:00. Some nights I know I drove her crazy because I was on and off my bedpan every time she turned around.

She was kind to me. She never complained about me needing her help at anytime during the night. She and I would talk on the nights I could not sleep; I would get up and get in my wheelchair and go out into the hall. She would want to know if I was alright. Most of the time, I was awake because of the pain, so she would check my pain medicine with the nurse and see if it was time for another dose. The nurse would bring it to me.

I tried not to bother my CNAs at night, so I never got to know most of the CNAs that worked this shift.

CHAPTER TEN

Special Visitors

Faithful Family

Jim and Gary

My husband, Jim, and our cousin, Gary Lewis, who we call our brother, both came to see me almost every weekend. Some weekends it looked like they were moving in, when our Aunt Kaky sent things to them to bring me and my friends. Jim would bring me things I needed; sometimes he brought me flowers.

As I improved, we were able to go to the dining room for lunch where they got to eat free. We all enjoyed the food.

I treasured every week; their visits were part of what helped keep me going. It was always hard to see them leave. I cannot tell you how many times I wanted to get in the van and go home.

My Big Brother, Dell Stewart

I treasured my last visit on Thanksgiving Day when Dell came with my husband, Jim, for lunch. We ate with my friend, Tim, and we all enjoyed the day.

It was the beginning of the hardest time in our lives, not knowing when or if Dell and I would see each other again, since he was facing chemo treatments for his colon cancer. They had removed the tumor and part of his colon, and were going to do chemo to be on the safe side.

After the Thanksgiving trip, we did not get to see each other again until I got home on February 23, 2005. All we could do was talk on the phone. We prayed for each other.

That Thanksgiving Day was a day to be very thankful, and we were.

Faithful Friends

My Pastor, Larry Bagby, and My Friend, Twila Slezak

Larry and Twila came to see me a couple of times. We enjoyed our visits. We laughed and sang gospel songs together. Larry knows how I love to talk, so we talked and talked, and guess what? He listened!

Larry and Twila would call and see how I was doing, asking me what was going on. We always prayed, for we knew there is power in prayer.

Their calls, visits, concern, kindness, friendship, thoughtfulness and most of all, love, meant so much to me and my loved ones.

A faithful friend is a sturdy shelter. He that has found one has found a treasure and that's Larry and Twila.

Connie Barton, Rita Gorth, Suzy Dunagan

My long-time friend, Connie Barton, whom I had worked for at her hair salon, Styles by Ja-Co-Pay for 15 years; Connie's sister, Rita Gorth; and their sister-in-law, Suzy Dunagan, came to see me one afternoon. They all brought me a gift. We visited and talked and laughed. Connie told me she had brought her scissors; they were in the car. I replied, "What are they doing in your car? Go get them!"

So she went and got them, she put a cape around my neck, and she had to stand behind my bed to cut my hair, which was not easy—it took awhile. It helped me feel so much better!

We enjoyed the rest of our visit. It was good to see all of them. It had been a while since we had seen each other.

Jamie Brown, Martha Walls, Sandy Peeler and Libby

I worked at Justinian's for almost ten years—these were just a few of the girls that came to see me. Jamie Brown I had worked together for 25 years. We had worked at her shop, Styles by Ja-Co-Pay for 15 years, plus ten years at another shop called Justinian's.

Sandy Peeler, Martha Walls and I worked not quite ten years together at Justinian's; Libby started working there after I retired on disability. All four of them brought me gifts—we are gift-giving people.

I was lying on my wedges on my left side when they surprised me, so two of them sat on the side of my bed with me and the other two found a seat. We laughed and talked, and I introduced them to my friend Bill and a few other friends and staff. We got a kick out of Bill. We enjoyed our visit and then we said our good-bye's.

Special Thanks

Aunt Kaky Jones (Kathleen)

Words cannot express my appreciation to Aunt Kaky. She was not able to come visit me while I was in Jackson,

Tennessee, but she called me all the time. She made sure to check on me in every situation. She brought all kinds of food and things to Jim, so when he came on the weekends to visit me, I never knew what all he was bringing us.

Sometimes he brought diet drinks in cans or two-liter bottles. Aunt Kaky sent popcorn, regular and diabetic sugar-free candy, crackers, animal cookies, peanut butter and crackers, cheese crackers and homemade cakes. One time I mentioned wanting one of her pound cakes, and the next weekend I got one.

She also sent a sour cream coconut cake which we ate at activity one day. Everyone got a piece; it was delicious! She even sent me a container of condiments like mayonnaise, mustard and ketchup, and salad dressing for my salads. She knew how Tim and I liked our peanut butter, so she sent that too. She always sent enough so I could enjoy sharing with my friends and the staff.

All the things you did, Aunt Kaky, made me feel like you were with me. You were in my heart and you will always have a special place in my life.

Thanks for everything, but most of all for loving me as your niece and for being my Aunt Kaky.

Tributes

Mother

God, take care of my mother.
You would be proud of your loving daughter.

With God's love, I no longer need food for help.
He's taught me how precious love is.
Now I can love me, others and life itself.

A mother's love is precious.
A father's love is supreme.

Together they are forever
In His loving home.

> *Love,*
>
> *Your Daughter,*
>
> *Regina Kinney*

Dear Daddy

I am sorry for the pain I have caused you.
I never meant to hurt you and
To have you be the way you were
In your last years of life.

I have to really, really let go of the times
We hated each other, and what we
Were doing to each other.

For I was stubborn, and our lives together
Could have been different if we were
Not so determined to not let go of our anger.
I'm sorry we let our anger keep us
From loving each other like we should have.

I know you and Mom had to love each other
Or the two of us children would not
Have been brought into this world.

Now that the two of you are with God in heaven,
Your children look forward to the day we join you.
And today we want to say again how much we love
And appreciate all you have done for us in our lives

Love,
Regina, Dell & Jim

My Soul Mate

I prayed for a long time
For God to send me someone
Who would be special in my life
You Jim are my friend
And the lover of my life.
I didn't realize until
We were apart for eight months
What we had together.
Thanks for all you do
All your understanding ways,
And for loving me in such
A special way.

For God knew better than
We did that our love
Would grow, the more
We grew in His love.

Someday we will be in the
Beautiful clouds and stars
With our Heavenly Father
And our families
All together
In His love forever.

Love You, Sweetheart

Stinker

Thank you God for protecting and watching over Carole, we lovingly call our "Stinker." Thank you for preserving her during Hurricane Katrina and bringing her back to us safely at that time. Hurricane Katrina made us wake up and appreciate how very fragile and precious life is. Carole, your dad and I love you very much. Never forget that.

Love,

Dad and Momma Regina

My Penny from Heaven

Not having been a mother,

There was always something lacking in my life

Until I received my "Penny from Heaven."

God used Penny to show me how fulfilling

The role of a mother is.

I found a treasure that will last forever.

Love,

Dad and Mom Regina

Mom's Children

Dear Children,
Mom believes in you,
Mom thinks you are great,
Mom loves you,
You have Mom's approval
And Mom's blessing forever.
(Matthew 19: 13-14)

Love to All My Children,

Mom

My Big Brother

When life was full of pain and sorrow
You cared and loved your little sister.
And no other can compare to my big brother.
You'll always be special to
Your little sister, Genie.
I love you my big brother, Dell.

Love,

Your Little Sister Regina (Genie)

Godmother

Our Mama Bea is an angel heaven sent to each of
us children.

She loves and cares for us; there is not

A time she doesn't worry about us.

She is always praying for us, checking up on us

And making sure that we are all right.

God put Mama Bea in each of our lives to have a

Mother while all of ours are in heaven waiting on

Us to arrive when God calls each of us home.

Until then, she continues to take us in her wings

And be our godmother whom we will love forever
in eternity.

Your Children Love You,

Regina and Jim

My Dearest Pat

Thanks for putting us in each other's lives;
We are very close, the sister I never had.
We tell each other everything
We can pray, cry, laugh, talk and depend on
Each other at all times.
We love our friendship; we love each other;
When one hurts the other hurts.
We feel each other's pain and sorrow.
We have been through so much with the
Loss of loved ones, our mom, our dads,
Our Terry and we have that
Blessed assurance we will see them all
In our heavenly home someday.
That is what keeps us at
Peace and rest.

Love,
Sister Regina

Hairstylists

Hairstylists have a special love for people,
We understand all different walks of life.
We hear it all; there is nothing that can shock us.
We hear things that people would never
Tell anyone else. We learn not to judge
Anyone. We know we are all human beings
And that we are all put in this life
For a reason.
Hairstylists have some of the biggest hearts
And we understand life.
We love people and people love us.
We know people's pain and sorrow,
We know how to have fun, joy and laughter.
We truly love our job; it brings us
As much satisfaction as we do to our
Customers. They are more than just
Customers, they are family who we
Will love forever.

> *My love to*
> *All Hairstylists and Customers,*
> *Regina*

Friends

Friends are always there when you need them.

You can tell a good friend your most important things in life.

When I think of all my friends I think of how God has blessed my life with so many who are more than friends.

They are family and I treasure each of you, dear friends.

Your Loving Friend,

Regina

Wonderful Life Friends

My wonderful life friend came to me at a
time when he and I both needed a friend.
Tim had lost his dear wife and I was away
from my family for the longest and hardest
six months of my life. Tim and I became best
friends and we ended up being the family that we
both needed during this painful time in our lives.
Now we continue our journey away from
each other until God brings us both
to heaven to live in eternity with
Him and there we will remain as
wonderful life friends forever.

Love,

Your Wonderful Friend, Regina

Poems for Life

God Holds the Key

God holds the key,
He takes care of your problems.
Always talk to Him about your problems
And never ask Him "Why?"

God holds the key, always be positive,
One touch from Him and He can change everything.
With God all things are possible.

God holds the key, He opens doors,
Dreams come true because God holds the key.

God Is in Control

On this Tuesday morning
As I talk to my God
As I look up in the clouds,
I now understand why God is
Always everywhere and
How He loves us so.

Look up, look up, my friends
If you don't know
Him as your personal Savior.

My children, you are
Missing the most
Precious gift
Of our Heavenly Father.

Waiting for the Railway

(To Jim & Dell from your wife and little sister)

Waiting on the "Big Boy" –
The biggest train ever made.

My husband and brother, Jim and Dell,
They are like two little boys
Waiting on Santa Claus
To bring them a new little toy.

They are so impatient
You would think Christmas
Would never arrive.

Just waiting on the "Big Boy" for them
Was like waiting on Santa when they were small.
Today, the two can hardly wait for the train to arrive.

Author of Life

Jesus was taken up to heaven
And a cloud hid Him.
He will return
For all of us someday.

Only the Father knows the
Time of His return.
God made it clear that the Messiah
Had to suffer, and Jesus made it
Come true on the cross.

Salvation is to be found through Him alone
For there is no one else in all the world
Whose name God has given to men
By whom we can be saved.

Jesus said I will see you again and
Your heart will be filled with gladness,
The kind no one can take away from us.

The author of life is alive and
Will return to take
Us home forever.

Walking in the Spirit

I am walking with
The Spirit of God within me.
I'll never walk alone
For He fills my soul
Deep in my spirit.
He brings me love, joy and peace
In all I do and say.
I am truly living the life
He has planned For His child.

Full Tank of Gas

Going to church is like going
To the service station to
Get a full tank of gas.
God can fill you with His Holy Spirit;
Let Him be your full tank of gas.

Knock, Knock

Knock, knock.
"Who's there?
God.

I pray you don't have to ask "God who?"
If you do, I pray for your lost soul.

You need to pray, and ask God to come into
Your heart and soul.

Ask and ye shall receive.

God Is Our Pilot

Before God becomes our pilot,
We are not honorable in the car.
God, be our pilot.

Before God becomes our pilot,
We treat others on the highway as enemies.
God, be our pilot.

With God as our pilot
We don't have to worry about road rage.
We are kind to everyone
And our trip becomes enjoyable.

God took our fears away
And we now arrive
In safety because we are in His hands.

Make it a habit to be kind, polite and thoughtful,
To others, smile and wave.
Check your spirit before getting in the driver's seat
For it's His life He gave.

Remember to slow down
And stop being in a hurry.
Let God be your pilot
And you will not worry.

Grace of Life

Use your step of faith
Believe in God,
He directs our steps,
He puts us where He wants us to be.

Trust Him and be on the lookout
God is behind the scenes,
He will bring joy in your circumstances
Exercise faith and He will give you the grace of life.

My Heavenly Father

My Heavenly Father is always with me
He is the delight of my world.
He brings me joy
His arms are always open to me.

I come to Him, He's my Rock and Redeemer.
He is my Heavenly Father and
I am His child.
I am His special treasure, His jewel.

He's my Heavenly Father
And we have special love like no other.

God's Signature

God chose you,
We are who we are.
Walk with Him,
He wants only you.
You need God's signature,
He gave you life.
So take His hand and let Him write
Your name in His Book of Life.
You are a divine work of art.

God's Eyes

God sees us as His treasure,
He sees us as a source of joy,
He sees our value.

God looks at our hearts,
Looking for us to be pure at heart.

Look for God's eyes
And you'll find your treasure,
Your joy and
Your value in Him.

The Presence of God's Joy

God's presence brings us joy in smiling, laughing
Listening to music, singing and dancing.

To experience joy God has given us
A well of living water in our spirit.

God's presence will give you a gusher
Of living water that will overflow, to the fullest.

So enjoy God's presence of joy in loving.

What's Ahead

Life is only a moment
Live by faith.
God, protect us for what's ahead.

Trust the Lord with all your heart,
And don't depend on your own understanding.
Depend on Him for what's ahead.

God's Morning

When I rise up in the early hours
I'm satisfied with God's mercy
And loving-kindness in the morning.

When I rise up in the morning
I'll rejoice and be glad in it.
When I rise up in the morning
I'll slow down and enjoy the day
With His love for today.

Treasured Friend

When He found me, I was in the pits of hell.
He brought this sinner to a sturdy shelter
And now I have a treasured friend.

He's my treasured friend
For all eternity.

Swept Away

God is ready to strengthen us,
Cling to His promise and You will not stumble.

Reach up to your Father, He will hold your hand,
The storm is in His all-powerful hands.
Be swept away by His love and faithfulness,
Just hear His "Peace be still."

Cradle

Cradled in the arms of His great love
We find peace, rest and great satisfaction
Knowing all is well.

For He cradles us through all life's battles
And we find victory in Him.
Let God cradle you forever.

Open Hands

Surrender and go to God's open hands,
He has set you free to be His children.

Let Him govern not by law but by love
With His open hands.

We are truly free
Walking with the Savior.

Our Nation Needs to Turn to God

This nation is broken-hearted
And has lost the spirit of God.
As a nation we need to put the
Love back in our hearts and spirits.
God is an awesome God
He can be in everyone's spirit again
If only you'll let Him.
He knows our hurts,
Our disappointments and grief.
He can make a way where there is no other.

Open your heart and spirit to
His loving hands.
Only He can heal our nation
And make loving memories
That we can take to our heavenly home forever.

Purpose of Life

Love the Lord your God with all your heart,
Soul, mind and body.

Acknowledge your God-given talents
He put them there for us to enjoy, so we
Could always have a purpose in life.

Look for God to help you find
The reason you are here and what
His purpose is for your life.

He'll make a way like no other can.
Learn to love your purpose in life
In all you do and say, and thank Him.

Your Whispering Thoughts

Give God your whispering thoughts,
Thank Him for every breath with
Your whispering thoughts.

Whisper in the morning
Whisper in the afternoon,
Whisper in the evening
Whisper to sleep.

God knows all your thoughts
So keep on whispering to Him in your thoughts.

At His Feet

God knows we have fallen
Lay down your cares at His feet.
Give Him all your anxieties
Only He will not turn away from you.
So cast your cares at His feet
He will give you hope and a life of eternity.

God's Perfect Plan

God's perfect plan puts us where
He wants to take us.

With a life of love, joy, peace, patience, kindness,
Goodness, faithfulness, gentleness and
Self-control,

We live only but a moment
In His perfect plan and we will be
In His presence for all eternity.

(Galatians 5:22-23-paraphrased)

Apple

We are His children and the apple of His eye,
And He is our Loving Father.
He is my apple of life, mind, body and soul.

It makes me want to sing.
He's my apple in the morning
He's my apple in the afternoon
He's my apple in the evening
He's my delight in all things.

God's Fight

Let God fight for you,
His job is to fight for you.
Stay calm and believe and trust God.

So pray and wait
For He is always fighting the battles
For His children.

When God's on your team you are a winner,
He is my defender.
I will not be defeated.

(Psalm 62:6)

Simple Life

*With God in our lives we can
Find the love, peace, rest and
All we need to have a simple life.*

*A simple life is filled with the strength of God.
He is our source of life.
Your treasure is where your heart is.*

Your Comfort Delights My Soul

*My soul finds comfort and delight
Every day of life with hope and joy.*

*As I live and breathe in life with every precious
Moment God gives me comfort and
Delight in my soul.*

*God keeps me and guides me and I delight in Him
"The heavens declare the glory of God."*

(Psalm 19:1)

God's Loving Hands

With God's loving hands I can make a
Delicious dessert for He is my helper.
I put love and enjoyment in every
Baked goody that comes from
My sweet and loving kitchen
With God's loving hands.

Our Safe Haven

Our safe haven is in the arms of God,
He loves us and we are
His treasure and precious jewels.

God is our protection. Run to Him, let Him
Cover you with His graciousness no
Matter what your needs or wants are.

He knows your pain, sorrow, anger and
Grief so let Him be your safe haven
And you will have touched a little bit of heaven.

No Coincidence

No matter what race, creed or color a person is,
God created each of us in
His own image.
God put each of us in the world to love as He loved,
To care as He cares.
We don't have to wait till we have a problem
In our world to come to Him first.

He needs to always be first in our lives,
After all, He laid down His life for us.
If it weren't for Him we wouldn't be here.
It is no coincidence that we are here
Until He calls us home.

The Value of the Planted Seed

God watched over the seed that was planted.
One day it took root and grew
Until the day the Lord came into my heart.

Now I can lie down and go to sleep with
Peace in my heart, mind, body and soul
Knowing without a shadow of a doubt
That when I die I'll be with my
Heavenly Father forever.

Home in Heaven

Our home in heaven is where our Father is
Waiting for us to be under His roof. He's got
Our place set at His table.

He longs to be with us as we do Him.
When the time is right He'll call us home
And we'll be amazed in all we see and do.

There will be more joy and happiness
Than we have ever experienced in our lifetime.

At last, we'll see His face and get that
Precious time in His presence for all eternity.

Ask Christ for His Address

God gives us what no other gives us,
God gives us grace.

God never fails. That's what makes
God the Almighty.

Invite Jesus to take up residence in your heart,
He's the greatest Love you'll ever know.

God Is in Your Home

*God came into my home on the night that
I lost it. I was totally fed up with life.
I was in my wheelchair, my husband was in his
recliner, my best friend was in a chair next to me.*

*I decided to call another friend and this
was the best phone call I ever made.
My friend knew the pain I was in, so she
asked me to ask the Lord to come into my life.*

*This was the best feeling I have ever experienced,
The power of God's Spirit filled me with
the Holy Spirit and I'll never be the same.
Praise God I am a new creature and I thank
God He came in my home and brought me into
His family forever. Life is wonderful!*

As God Sees Me

It took God's love for me to allow
His love to change the way I see me.

I learned to see me as God sees me,
He loves me and now I also love me.

He sees me as a person who loves and
Cares for people's feelings.
Now when you hurt I feel your pain.

God has given me many talents and
He brings the best out in all of them.

My ability to cook and bake goodies is better
When I call upon His help.

He has given me the ability to write poems,
Short stories, and so far two books for which I give
Him all the glory and honor.

"Every good and perfect gift is from God"
(James 1:17).

Only God Can Heal Your Heart

God healed me down in my gut and heart,
Only He can truly save and heal you
From all of life's hurt and pain.

Let go and let God heal you in your gut,
Praise Him continually for your healing.

132

Christ Lives in Me

On the night the Lord came into my life
Christ lived in me,
He made my heart His home.
I now have within me a portion of the very
Thoughts and mind of Christ.
I thank Christ for living in me.

Midst of the Storm

God came to me in the midst of my storm,
He was waiting for me to call on Him.

He knew I was tired,
Had heavy loads and needed rest.

He brought me comfort and
Peace out of the storm.

God Sees Me

God sees me as His child whom
He loves and who He wants to
Succeed in everything I set
My mind to do.

He sees me writing lots of soul-winning
Books, poems, songs and movies.

God sees me prosperous,
God sees me a size that I
Will be very proud of.

God sees a giving and loving person in
This child of His.

Who I Am

I can't be the person people want me to be,
I can only be who He created me to be—
And that's more than good enough

The truth doesn't stop
Me from hurting, when people
Act as though I'm not worth their
Time and energy.

Please take away the pain of rejection
Comfort me now with the truth
About how valuable and loved I really am.

My body was made for the love of God,
Every cell in my body is a hymn
To my Creator...
And that's who I am.

Turn Back to God

Turn back to God and seek
Him in your life.

God loves all of us,
He cares what happens to all of us too much to let
Us aimlessly wander through life
Without meaning or purpose.

We need to ask God to be an instrument
Of His love to those around us.
God grant us life, expect it, declare it,
Only He can open or close doors.

We need a touch from God.
We need to walk in His love
And we can live in victory forever.

God Opens and Shuts Doors

God opens and shuts doors for a reason
Only He can give us rest and peace in our lives.
He puts a smile on our faces.

Keep pressing forward
And know that God is in control of your circumstances.
You can rise above everything.

Let God open and shut doors
Trusting Him whether you get your way or not.

You'll have victory while seeking the
Kingdom of heaven
While letting Him open and shut doors.

Keeping Our Mouths Shut

*It's better to keep our mouths shut
Than to say words that we may regret.*

*Words that hurt will leave scars we
May carry in our lives for years
And will cause deep-rooted problems.*

*Put your words in God's control,
Obey Him and then He will put the
Right words that will heal all
The deep-rooted problems.*

Serious About Our Christian Walk

*God wants us all to get serious about
Our Christian walk with Him.*

*Learn to love God as your Father, Daddy, Abba,
As He loves us as His children, and do it
With the same passion He has for us.*

*God wants us to get serious with His Holy Spirit
Where we become fruit that produces
Love, peace, patience, kindness, goodness,
Faithfulness, gentleness and self-control.*

*God wants us to get serious with His words
And to learn to listen to them as He does us.*

*God wants us to get serious to learn His will
For our lives and to know His timing is perfect
And to always walk in His way.*

Will of God

Serve God's will and your heart
Will know all is well.

Stop staying in bondage
Be in God's will.

Getting free comes when
You are in the will of God.

Let your flesh kick up a fit and
It will be your will not God's.

(John 6:37-38)

God Is Watching

Learn to see God as He sees you
Allow His love to change the way
You look at yourself.

God will put love in your heart
So you can truly love yourself.

Let Him live long enough in a heart
And that heart will begin to change.

He has such high aspirations for youGod envisions
a complete restoration.

He won't stop until He is finished
He wants us to be like Jesus.

Scars into Stars

Give your scars to God
Give your scars to God
We all make mistakes
So be willing to forgive yourself.

Give your scars to God
Give your scars to God
Don't live in regret.

Give your scars to God
Give your scars to God
Live by faith.

Give your scars to God
Give your scars to God
He will turn scars into stars.

A Hungry Heart

Worship Him with a hungry heart
Worship Him with a hungry heart.

Come let us worship Him and bow down
Let's kneel before the Lord who has made us.

Worship Him with a hungry heart
Worship Him with a hungry heart
Only He can fill a hungry heart.

Worship Him and He'll get you home,
He will get you home and there your hungry heart
will be filled.

Just Like Heaven

Life on Earth can be just like heaven,
God can do everything to make
Your life here on Earth as
Wonderful as heaven.

Let God lead your life where
He leads you, He will take you to
Places you never dreamed of.

With God's love your love will
Be heaven-sent.

We are here only a moment doing
What He has planned for our lives
Until He takes us to Heaven.

God's Child

I am a child of God
We are friends, we talk to each other
We hear each other and
He answers His child.

Only God can lead me where I need to be led.
I am the apple of His eye
And He is the delight of my life.
Therefore, I am God's child.

Never Too Late

*It's never to late to take up His cross.
The Lord knows all and when we
Realize this we know it's never too late.
Ask and ye shall receive His love.*

*For God loved the world so much
That He gave his only Son so that
Anyone who believes in Him shall
Not perish but have eternal life.*

(John 3:16)

I Pray You Have the Key

*We all have keys to our car and house
I pray you have the key
To open the door to heaven.*

*If not, pray with me, Lord,
I pray for my lost soul, come into my life,
Lord, I need that key to
Open Your heavenly door.*

Amen.

Love

There's no better love than the love of God.
He cares for all of us
He provides us with all the love we need.

He gives us the rest we need and
The peace we need for everyday.
Let God's love be over all you do and say
And there will be no greater love.

24/7

My first thought is Him in the morning when I rise
Praising Him for a good night's rest
Knowing He's watching over me as I sleep.

As I live and breathe, walk, see, hear,
Feel and touch my world,
I know God is with me in all I do and say.

He's my 24/7 God, not my Sunday-box God
Where He only hears from me on
Sunday morning in worship service.

Trouble

Take God at His word
Only He can help you with your trouble.

Believe in God and take Him in your heart
And your trouble will be taken away and
Never be remembered again.

Praise Him, praise Him!
God is our Redeemer, life and love forever.

Choices

God said give Me your firstfruits
And everything shall be added unto you who seek Me
And you will have the Kingdom of God.

Give your time to God, He will take you off that
Broad path and life will be easier.

Give your flesh to God and
He'll change your choices.

God's grace will bring you out of all
Your problems and His grace
Will fill you with His Holy Spirit.

142

Bread of Life

Go to God,
He who comes to Him
Will never be hungry,
He who believes in Him
Will never be thirsty.

God will be your Bread of Life
And you will always
Be full of life.

(John 6:31-35; John 6:47-51)

Finding Passion for God

God is looking for all of us to
Find our passion for Him.

Be yourself and God will help
You find your passion for Him.

God has a fire for us,
He knows our motives.
Only He can help us find
Our passion for Him.

Praise God for His passion
And love for all of us.

Passion for Prayer

There is power in prayer,
God loves to hear from us through prayer,
He wants us to find passion in prayer.

Pray and surrender all to Him
With your passion for prayer
And He'll answer and bless you
In all you do and say.

Life Is a Dash

We are brought in this world to
Live the best life we can.

Life is only a dash
We are here for only a moment
And gone the next.

With God in our lives
We'll live forever with Him
In the home He has made for you.

Everything Belongs to God

When we learn that everything we have
Is not ours but God's,
We learn to trust everything
God has in store for our lives.
God has endowed us with all our talents,
They are God-given, so we will do the best
With what He's given us.
Let's enjoy all God has for our lives.

Encouraging Words

We all need to be encouraged.

Let me encourage you to read His Word,
Learn His Word, live His Words and to
Give others encouraging words with love

Let me encourage you to have
A special relationship with God.

Life in My Wheelchair

I surrender my life to the Lord
In my wheelchair.

I thank God for my broken pelvis
Which is what it took for me to need
Him in my life.

God brought me through all my life's problems
And He put that love in my heart so I could truly love.

Let God Be Light and Living Water

Live in the light of the world and
You'll never walk in darkness.

Only God can truly fill our thirst
With His stream of living water.

(John 8:12-20; John 7:37-39)

Hold On

Hold on to your dreams
God can and will make all
Dreams come true.

God put a seed in your life and
He will bring your dreams to life.

Our God is the Way-maker.
Sing a song of praise in your heart.
Get happy feet and He'll turn things around in your favor.
Can you hear God blessings and favor?
Thank Him for victory coming your way.
God is the Most High God
Hold on to your dreams.
Never let go of God's dreams,
He will make a way
When there is no other way.

Master Teacher

God and I are one;
God and you are one.

We are all one with God and
One in Spirit with one another.

This puts our life into rhythm,
Balance and coherence.

We are then integrated with all
Other human beings, with God
And with our universe.

"The Father and I are one" (John 10:30).

Unconditional Love

The truest love is unconditional.
This is the love Jesus modeled,
A love that God extends to everyone
Of us everyday and that will last forever.

Freely let God guide and
Freely God will share with us the
Wisdom and knowledge for
Living a happy and successful life.

With God we have greater meaning and purpose.
All that God is and all that God is capable
Of doing is for us every moment of our lives.

"As the Father has loved me, so I have loved you;
abide in my love" (John 15:9).

Action

God's love inspires us to the right action.
God's love sustains us spiritually and
Waters the depths of our souls.

With your guidance, I respect
All people and all creation.

Do all you do for the
Action of God
And give Him all the glory.

God Is So Good

God is so good, God is so good,
God has a plan for each of us.
He knows what we will be doing in our lives
He has a place and a purpose for each of us.

God is so good, God is so good,
Oh, God, our Helper in ages past.
He provides for all our needs
For God is so good.

The Capacity to Tap

*Seek the Kingdom of God
And you'll find the good.*

*God's love is His pleasure to give and
We all have the capacity to tap
Into His generosity.*

*The good you seek is seeking you
So don't be afraid, little flock.*

*For it gives your Father great
Happiness to give you the Kingdom.*

Sweet Mystery

*The sweet mystery of life
Is all around me.*

*The sweet mystery of life
Is the awesome presence of
God active in and through
All creation.*

*Realizing that others are
Living so splendidly by faith
Is a sweet mystery.*

Optional Love

The love of God is continually
Fulfilling every need I
Could ever have—even before
I am aware of a need.

I am provided for and loved
Loving one another isn't really optional,
It is what we are created to do.

In all that I do, I am free, for the
Spirit of God within me is my
Freedom to live fully and abundantly.

"Where the Spirit of the Lord is, there is freedom."
(2 Corinthians 3:17)

Risen Prayer

I know my prayers rise
Up to God and they are always
Returned with His blessing, for
He knows best.

I praise God for the return
Of my risen prayers
For He always answers.

Increase Our Faith

*Something each of us needs to do is
Increase our faith.*

*Cast your cares on the Lord and He will
Sustain you; He will never let the righteous fall.*

*The effects of the righteous will be quietness
And confidence forever.*

*Do not let your heart be troubled and
Do not be afraid.*

Lord, increase our faith.

Amen.

Wonders

Many, O Lord my God,
Are the wonders You have done.
The Lord your God is with you,
He is mighty to save.
He will take great delight in you,
He will quiet you with His love,
He will rejoice over you with singing.

Enjoy all His wonders!
I Am the Way, the Truth, the Life
Don't fall short from Jesus Christ.
Only He can show you
The Way, the Truth, the Life.

God will shine in all your life now and
He will open you to
The Way, the Truth, the Life.

Let it shine, Let it shine, Let it shine.

Joy

*For the joy of the Lord
is your strength.*

*Every good and perfect gift is
From above, coming down from
The Father of heavenly lights.*

*Set your mind on the things above,
Not on earthly things.*

*We have peace with God through
Our Lord Jesus Christ.*

*Commit to the Lord whatever you do.
Your plans will succeed and
You will find your true joy in this world.*

Wisdom

*If you lack wisdom, ask God
Who gives generously to all
Without finding fault, and
It will be given to you.*

*Wisdom that comes from Heaven
Is first of all pure, then peace-loving,
Considerate, submissive, full of mercy
And good fruit, impartial and sincere.*

Attitude of Trust

Live with an attitude of trust,
Cast your cares on the Lord.

Trust keeps you from worry and
Trying to figure out everything on your own.

Trust God in and through everything,
Only God can give you true trust.

A dedicated walk with God can
Change your trust to "Your will, not mine."

Through It All

God is so good, He brought our family
Through so much in our lifetime.

I thank Him for getting us
Through all our trials and tribulations.

I thank Him for carrying all our burdens
And for all He has done for us.

I love Him more and more with each passing day
And I look forward to the day He calls His child home.

Tomorrow

Yesterday was yesterday,
Today was today,
But tomorrow,
I do not boast about tomorrow.

For I don't know what a day may bring forth.
I look only on today,
And I look forward to my tomorrow
In heaven with my Lord.

Soul

Here in the quiet of my soul,
I am fully conscious of the love of Christ
And the order that His love sustains
Within me and all around me.

In life my soul has found the love, peace and
Satisfaction knowing when my soul leaves this earth
I will be in heaven with my Lord.

Imagine this awareness as I go about my daily life,
Praising Him all my days here on Earth.

It's Not All About Me

Life is not always about me.
God said to love Him first and your neighbor as yourself.

God can put this kind of love in all of us
If we would only let Him.

We are living in a world that is hurting
And thinking of ourselves.

Our God is the only one who can truly
Help our world and stop us from being so selfish.

Put God first and meditate on the Kingdom of God
We are to do His will, not our will.

Hasty Actions

Think about the consequences of our hasty actions,
They can cause more problems than they're worth.

Remember actions speak louder than words,
But words can sometimes harm more than they can help.

God leads us to say all the right things and only then
Will we not have to worry about these hasty actions.

Deliverance

God can take away all of life's problems
You ever had and truly deliver you into
His life of abundance.

Listen for His love and joy, and how precious
Life truly can be and you will know that
Someday you'll see Him face to face
In heaven for all eternity.

Cherish Life

Life is precious, cherish every moment,
For it could be our last, and if so
Cherish it knowing you will be in heaven and
Seeing Him face to face.

Life is worth cherishing, when we all get to
Heaven we will not only be with God, we will be
With our loving family forever.

God's Nails

We can only solve so many problems with
WD-40 and duct tape.

WD-40 can only loosen so much before
It loses its grip.

Duct tape can only tape and hold on so long
Before it falls apart.

We often try to fix problems with WD-40 and
duct tape but God did it with nails.

Put WD-40 and duct tape on your cross and
Let God carry your burdens.

God's Way

It is not the highway or byway, it is God's way,
It is the only way that will keep us from going to hell.
Choose God's way and He will lead you on the right path.

He said "I am the Way, the Truth, and the Life"
Which is the only way to live in
Heaven forever.

Destiny

If my God said it, I can have it.
I'm not a victim of anything.
I won't settle for less than my destiny.
I am complete but not completed.
I go with whom I can celebrate with.
I can be what God said I can be and
I want the greatest from God.

Never-failing God

It's about a wonderful life,
Living a relationship with a real, never-failing God.

We must get passionate for Jesus
Believing God for greater things than we can imagine.

God of hope, God of promise, God of miracles.
God is a never-failing God.

Sweet Words

How sweet are Your words to my taste!
Yes, sweeter than honey to my mouth.
You are my hiding place and my shield.
My words go up to You in prayer
And I await Your sweet words.

For they are the joy of my heart.
I shall delight in Your words.

I will not forget Your sweet words.
Lord Jesus, you said, "Heaven and earth will pass away,
but my words will never pass away" (Matthew 24:35).
Blessed are those who hear the Word of God and keep it.

"...he who hears My word, and believes in Him
who sent Me, has everlasting life, and shall not come into
judgment, but has passed from death into life."
(John 5:24 NKJ)

Twinkling of an Eye

In the twinkling of an eye
God came into my heart.
I will give thanks to You, O Lord
My God with all my heart and
Will glorify You forever.

Your lovingkindness toward me is great,
For You have delivered my soul from
The depths of hell.

Our Daily Cross

It is a new beginning,
Focus on taking up your daily cross,
Focus on Jesus and forget your past,
Lay your burdens down and your past on His cross
And move on to the life Jesus has designed for you.

We have to die daily, so we can focus on Jesus.
For Christ suffered on the cross for our sins
Which gives us freedom in Christ and great love for Him.

Take up your daily cross and live that life
Of joy and abundance that Jesus made available for you.

"Where the Spirit of the Lord is, there is freedom."
(2 Corinthians 3:17)

Open Your Heart to Jesus

Open your heart to Jesus,
Open your heart to Jesus,
Open your heart to Jesus.

Let Him fill the destiny of your life,
Only He can make the way.

Open your heart to Jesus,
Open your heart to Jesus,
Open your heart to Jesus.

Let His design fill your life
Only He can make the way.

Open your heart to Jesus,
Open your heart to Jesus,
Open your heart to Jesus.

Let Him fill your life with His love,
Only He can truly make a way.

Harmony

The only way we will ever live
Without conflict in our lives is to
Change our hearts to be like Jesus.
Only He can help us find harmony
To see only the good in one another—
Those created in His image.

The Greatest Gift

The greatest gift of life is living.
We are all one with God and
One in the spirit with one another.

God brought us all together in this world
To love one another, to care for one another
To truly want the best for one another.

His greatest love, the sacrifice of His Son,
Has given us the greatest gift.

That is living life to the fullest here and eternity with Him.
Life is precious and forever.

Clean Heart

The more good we open our hearts to,
The more good will flow into our lives,
And the more we will have to share
With one another.

My heart overflows with God's love.
He created in me a clean heart, O God,
And put a new and right spirit within me.

God is good and, as a result,
We are richly blessed with a clean heart.

Comfort

We need to learn to do one thing at a time,
And not worry about what others think of us.

Peace comes on purpose.
With God's will you'll find inner rest
For your soul.

Cast all your burdens on the Lord
For all things work for good
To those who love God.

Loyalty

Learn to be loyal to family and friends.
Believe the best in everyone.
Defend them, stick up for others and
Be there for them through thick and thin.

Be loyal in the toughest of times,
Be a true and loyal friend,
Restore him gently.

Pull together as friends and family.
He who pursues righteousness and
Loyalty finds life.

No Separation from God

"O Lord, nothing can separate us from Your love,
Neither death, nor life, nor angels, nor principalities,
Nor things present, nor things to come, nor power, nor
Height, nor depth, nor any other created thing can separate
us from Your love which is in Christ Jesus our Lord."
(Romans 8:38)

Through You we can do all things.
You shall supply all our needs
According to Your riches in glory.

Lord, we thank You that your Word promises us that
In Your Father's house are many dwelling places,
That You have gone to prepare a place for us, and
You will come again and receive us
Unto Yourself that where You are
We may be also.

God is always with us.

He Touched Me

He touched me through a life of obesity.
He touched me through an "open book" wound.
He touched me through the pain of a broken pelvis.
He touched me through the hole in my heart—He healed it.
He touched me through caregivers,
He touched me through therapy,
He touched me through family, friends and loved ones,
He touched me through all life's storms.
I'll never walk without His touch.

Amen

Journey

Life's Fulfilling Journey

Our journey in life starts with our first breath and from that moment on we meet our parents, brothers, sisters, all our family, friends and many special people who will come and go in our lifetime. Through my journey, there was so much pain from being close to verbal and physical abuse in my past.

In the midst of this journey, I graduated from high school and beauty school. I did hair for almost 30 years, finally got married at 40 years of age and became a wife, mother and grandmother in a single day.

Then my journey sent me on a road I thought was from hell. An accident put me in the hospital for two months and then six months in a healthcare facility away from my family to receive therapy for a broken pelvis.

On this journey, God sustained me. He knew that it would take this long, arduous journey to bring this child of His to Himself and it did.

My journey showed me that my God is the Shepherd who guides me, the Lord who provides for me, the Voice who brings me peace in the storms of life and the Physician who heals me.

I thank God for the journey I am on and the hardships that have formed me into what I am today. May I invite you to journey with God and give your life over to the Lord Jesus Christ? You only need to ask Him to forgive you of your sins and take complete charge of your life. You will experience joy and peace like you've never known before and your life will never be the same. May God continue to guide you in your own personal journey.